TOM MOORE'S DIARY

A SELECTION EDITED, WITH
AN INTRODUCTION, BY

J. B. PRIESTLEY

CAMBRIDGE
AT THE UNIVERSITY PRESS
MCMXXV

Republished, 1970
Scholarly Press, 22929 Industrial Drive East
St. Clair Shores, Michigan 48080

*STATE COLLEGE
LIBRARY*

FRAMINGHAM, MASS.

Library of Congress Catalog Card Number: 76-131783
Standard Book Number 403-00670-8

This edition is printed on a high-quality,
acid-free paper that meets specification
requirements for fine book paper referred
to as "300-year" paper

PRINTED IN GREAT BRITAIN

INTRODUCTION

I

A DIARY may give us a picture of a man or a picture of an age. The writer may turn his gaze inward, hardly troubling to record outward events, and describe his hot fits of passion and his cold fits of repentance, his bursts of pride, his frequent lapses into gloom and despair, in short, he may paint for us his heart and secret mind. If he does this, it does not matter who he was and when or where he lived; he has given us a document of great human interest. On the other hand, the diarist may be worlds away from such introspection and self-analysis, never looking within himself but looking outward at his times, describing, as truthfully as he can, his friends and acquaintances, his and their activities, the gossip and the anecdotes that reach his ears, and so forth, and so creating for us, stroke by stroke, a faithful portrait of his age. Such records are contributions to history, social, literary, political, and if they are at once lively and truthful, they are something more, they are good literature, to be enjoyed for their own sake. The really great diarists, like Pepys, contrive to give us both a picture of themselves and a picture of their age; their journals are equally attractive under either of the above heads; but such records are very rare. All the rest can be classified under one of our two divisions, although there is no line of demarcation and the divisions overlap. The Journal of Thomas

Moore, which he began in 1818 and kept, more or less faithfully, until his powers failed him in 1847, belongs to the second class of diaries; it is the picture of an age. Except in a few passages, when a domestic crisis stirs the depths, Moore does not examine himself, does not show us his heart and mind, but is content to tell us what he did, where he went, and what he heard. He is not writing, as so many diarists are, for his own secret satisfaction, but is deliberately composing a day-to-day autobiography, catching his history as it flies. When he appoints Lord John Russell his literary executor in his will, he mentions his Journal, which, with letters and other matter, will form the basis of "some kind of publication, whether in the shape of memoirs or otherwise, which may afford the means of making some provision for my wife and family." He has an audience in view, and selects his materials accordingly. Thus, long stretches of time, in which he is busy writing in his cottage, are passed over quickly; he tells us very little concerning his actual work, its initial conception, the details of its progress, and so forth. On the other hand, he does not omit a single figure of any importance he met during the period (striving always to remember exactly what they said, though, curiously enough, rarely describing them—throughout he starves our visual sense), and always skims the cream of the talk at the great houses he visited. But he is not what we might call a professional diarist, like Crabb Robinson, his contemporary. The latter, we feel, made his life serve his diary, and spent half his days tracking down great literary figures, notebook in hand.

For this reason he is of far greater service to the critic and biographer than Moore is. For facts and first-hand information concerning the figures of the Romantic Period, Crabb Robinson has no equal. But Moore, though he selected his material with one eye on his audience, did not make his life serve his diary but simply made his diary mirror his life. He is not so useful as Crabb Robinson but he is vastly more entertaining. Moreover, he pictures a whole period, in almost all its aspects, whereas Crabb Robinson portrays for us simply a group of literary men. Moore's chief faults are, first, that he is apt to concentrate his and our attention upon the wrong people, in short, that many of his swans are now geese and little geese at that; and, secondly, that he is far too prolix, burying his good things under loads of chit-chat. For this reason, there is probably no diary that gains more from a fairly drastic but judicious process of cutting and selecting than this of Moore's. There are some diaries that it would be monstrous to cut and compress; even if they are prolix, such prolixity is part of their character and through it they achieve their end. Thus, there is no sense in cutting Pepys, for either you want the whole Pepys to browse in or you do not want it at all; a potted Pepys is little or no use. But Moore's diary, I repeat, gains from being compressed. Moore was himself something of a politician, and was the friend of most of the great Whig politicians of his day, so that it naturally follows that his Journal gives us an enormous amount of political discussion and gossip, crumbs that Moore picked up at the tables of Bowood and Holland House. Now the period under review is already well covered by political diarists and Moore has little or nothing of value to add to their large store, so that all this political matter of his can be cut out without any loss. A great deal of the anecdotage, the sweepings of table-talk, can also be omitted without any injustice to either writer or reader. What is left then shines more brightly, and is more readily appreciated by the reader who wishes to enjoy rather than to explore and dig. The following selection, which amounts to not more than about a fifth part of the complete Journals that Moore left behind, is simply the cream of the diary. No single interest, except the political, represented in the original diary has been overlooked. We have here a complete picture of the life Moore lived and the kind of world he lived in, and the value of the picture to us, it is clear, depends upon the character and interest of that life and that world. These deserve a word to themselves.

II

In 1818, the year in which the diary begins, Thomas Moore was an extremely successful man of letters, indeed, after Scott and Byron, the most successful man of letters of his time. The year before, *Lalla Rookh* had been published and had proved an immense success. His songs, of which he had already published several volumes, were known everywhere. In addition, he had made a great deal of money and a considerable reputation by a succession of political squibs and satires, and such volumes as *The Fudge Family in Paris*. He had recently removed to Slopperton Cottage, Wiltshire, chiefly to be near Bowood, Lord Lansdowne's country house, where, as will be seen from the diary, he was a very frequent and very welcome guest. Indeed, he was a favourite everywhere. He was a troubadour to the Whig society of the Regency. (Although the dates of this Journal carry us beyond the Regency, Moore and his friends were not only *in* but *of* the Regency, its typical figures, and wherever they were, no matter what the year should be, *there* was still the Regency.) The men liked his wit and humour and fund of good spirits over a bottle. The women liked his trim, little figure, bright eyes and fluttering tenor voice. He was, by nature, a gregarious, convivial soul, a born diner-out in the great age of dining-out. He was an Englishman's idea of what an Irishman should be. That he was flattered by the attentions of the great there can be no denying, nor can it be denied that he might have been a greater figure in literature (that is, in what *we* call literature, for he was great enough in his own day) if he had thought less about Holland House and more about Parnassus, if his way of life had not driven him to think only of immediate triumphs, if he had not written with one eye fixed upon Lady Holland, Lord Lansdowne and the rest. "Mr Moore converts the wild harp of Erin into a musical snuff-box," growls Hazlitt, who had a knack of penetrating mere literary fashions. We are not concerned here with Moore's literary reputation, but something must be said about his reputation as a man. If his own time was, on the whole, too kind to him, both as a poet and a man, posterity has certainly been unkind. His mode of life may have been, and probably was, a mistake, but once we accept it, we must admit that, within its bounds, he showed a manly independence that makes him something very different from the tuneful lap-dog of common report. Indeed, if we compare his conduct with that of most of the other poets of his time, poets who, unlike Tom Moore, were always talking morality, he cuts no mean figure. He neither accepted a pension for his change of opinion, nor lived on other people's allowances, nor let strangers keep his wife and family. His wealthy friends frequently pressed him to accept their help, but he always refused. When the deputy registrar he had left at Bermuda suddenly embezzled £6000, for which Moore was responsible, Moore had to leave England and make his home in Paris (hence the frequent entries dated from there during the years 1820–2) to escape a debtor's prison; but despite all offers of help from friends, he preferred to make an arrangement with his publishers to pay off the debt. Nor must the superficial appearance of ease and gaiety in his memoirs or in any accounts of him, in which this aspect of his life is always stressed, blind us to the fact that his life had its share, and perhaps more than its share, of anxiety, hard work, and domestic tragedy. He passes very lightly, as I have said, over the periods when he was slaving away at his biographies, political satires and the like, for weeks on end at his cottage. He was fortunate in having the best wife ("Bessy") that a man could possibly have, and though he was frequently forgetful and sometimes selfish (like most husbands with good wives), he was on the whole a very affectionate and devoted husband and father.

There is nothing better in the whole diary than the occasional glimpses we get of his domestic life, and now and then he writes of his wife in words that move us more than whole volumes of his love poetry. So too he was a fond father, and his last years, before his final collapse, were spent battling against debts that had been incurred on behalf of his children, not one of whom lived to benefit by his care. It is one of the ironical strokes common in this world that this couple, so devoted, so happy in their parenthood, should outlive all their children. Tom Moore had his day, and rattled it with the best of them, with his hair "curling in long tendrils" and his eyes sparkling "like champagne bubbles," with every poem a triumph, with tears and laughter and applause always at his command, the idol of a whole populace, the darling of a notable society; but, in spite of appearances, he was something more than a bright little singing-bird in a gold cage, fed on rose petals and for ever smoothed down by white hands; he had his life to live in this world and brought to the task and the adventure a stout heart and a manly spirit, and so was only defeated in the end by an old age that was assaulted by disaster after disaster.

III

Times change and with them opinion, and now we would rather have had Mary Lamb as our hostess than Lady Holland, would rather have had Charles Lamb's invitation to play whist and smoke a pipe than have had a score of dinners at Holland House. Nevertheless, we need not be blind to the fact that Holland House was the centre of an extremely brilliant society, a society that may have been slow to recognise great genius (and what society is not?) but that was saturated with wit and learning and literature, and made table-talk into an art. This was the society in which Tom Moore was at home, and his Journal is probably the best record of it we now possess. Nor was it the only society in which he found himself. In truth, he went everywhere. He will be found at Holland House at night, with the Whig statesmen, wits and men of letters, and will be breakfasting the following morning with Mary Shelley. He listens to Byron in Italy, Scott at Abbotsford, Wordsworth in London, Lafayette in Paris, and himself in Kilkenny. A lost age springs to life again in these pages. Byron, Scott, Wordsworth, Coleridge, Lamb, Rogers, Campbell, and a host of others, pass and repass. The publishers and editors come and go, making their suggestions and naming their figures. Sidney Smith, Luttrell, Jekyll, and the wits, crowd the dining tables again, turning their epigrams. "Gentleman Jackson," the boxer, calls to ask where the line "Men are but children of a larger growth" comes from, as there is a bet depending upon it. Young Macaulay, springing from nowhere, suddenly bursts upon the diners. We hear a discussion on the subject of "Boz, the new comic writer." We see Moore and Luttrell so overcome with laughter at Sydney Smith that when they arrive at Cockspur Street, all three are "obliged to separate, and reel each his own way with the fit." And best of all, we are given a glimpse, now and then, of Tom with his Bessy, of whom Maurice Hewlett (who put this diary

INTRODUCTION

to good uses) has written so exquisitely. "Through all the sparkle and flash," Hewlett writes, "under all the talk, through all the tinklings of pianos and guitars which declare Tom's whereabouts, if you listen you can hear the quiet burden of her heart-beats." What could be better, more revealing, than that early entry which describes how Moore read *The Vicar of Wakefield* to Bessy, who was recovering from a confinement, in the evening, and how there had come a young Irishman to the door who had said that his wife was delivered of twins on the road and was lying, without any comforts, at a neighbouring cottage, and how Bessy gave him a large jug of caudle, some clothes, tea, sugar, and money, and how they discovered, next day, that "'twas all a cheat" and, with a sigh, began their reading of *The Vicar of Wakefield* again. The whole episode might have come out of *The Vicar of Wakefield*. There may be readers who do not wish to learn that on April 1st, 1819, Tom Moore "made Bessy turn her cap awry in honour of the day," or that at eight o'clock of the 13th of May following, she and Tom sauntered up and down Burlington Arcade, then went and bought some prawns and supped "most snugly together"; but if there are such readers, we can only pity them and point out that there are great names and matters of more apparent moment elsewhere in the Journal. And if Moore's worth as a man and a husband should still be doubted, there is a little entry towards the end of the diary that of itself should clear all doubts. Moore simply tells us how, once again, he has played his old trick upon Bessy, for he has got a friend to send her a five-pound note as if it was his own gift and not Moore's for her supplies for the local poor. "It makes her happy without the drawback of knowing it comes from my small means, and, in the way she manages it, does a world of good." It is doubtful if any diary can show us anything more moving than Moore's description of the death of his little daughter, Anastasia, when the last thing that Bessy did before the coffin was closed "was to pull some snowdrops herself and place them within it." Poor Bessy, most unfortunate of mothers, there were yet other tragedies before her. Both her sons died when they had only just arrived at manhood, and one of them, Tom, their darling, after costing his father a small fortune and his mother a great many tears, died in disgrace, with the Foreign Legion. She was all mother, this Bessy, and yet she was driven to cry: "Why do people sigh for children? They know not what sorrow will come with them." Moore's last years were saddened by these repeated losses. His sister died, then his remaining son, and he writes: "The last of our five children is now gone, and we are left desolate and alone. Not a single relative have I now left in the world!" This selection ends before the final period, when, broken by these domestic tragedies, harassed by the task, for which he was not fitted, of compiling his *History of Ireland*, his powers gradually failed and the scattered entries in the Journal show more and more traces of a fading memory and a weakening hold upon life. These last entries make mournful reading and we can well spare them, now that Time has huddled away him and his friends and his enemies and all their days. It is better to watch the age being revived at its brightest, see Rogers sitting down to breakfast with his poets and politicians, or the footmen throwing open the doors while the beauty and wit and learning of England pass into Holland House.

J. B. PRIESTLEY

NOTE. The text of this selection is that of the 1860 edition of *The Memoirs, Journal and Correspondence of Thomas Moore*, edited by Lord John Russell. The spelling throughout is Moore's own. As frequent notes would be unwelcome in an edition of this kind, I have put in as few as possible, and these for the most part only refer to persons who were Moore's closest friends and who constantly make their appearance in his Journal. As most of these persons are well-known figures, the majority of readers will probably not require even such notes as there are, but they may help a few readers to understand and enjoy the text. It will be noticed that I have omitted to include Moore's account of one of the most famous incidents in his life, namely, the negotiations connected with Byron's "Memoirs" and their final destruction. The facts are simple and are to be found in all Byron literature. On the other hand, the negotiations were long and intricate, and Moore's account of them is very long and involved and very dull. This being so, and space being valuable, I have omitted the whole transaction and take this opportunity of apologising to those few readers who would rather not be without it.

A SELECTION FROM TOM MOORE'S DIARY

August 24 Arrived at my cottage. Always glad to return to it, and the dear girl who makes it so happy for me. Found heaps of letters, some of them from poets and authors, who are the pest of my life:—one sending me a "Serio-Comic Drama of Invasion, in Three Acts, including the Vision and the Battle," and referring me for his poetic credentials to three admirals and "the late comptroller of the navy." Another begging to know whether I was acquainted with "any man or woman to whom money was for a time useless," who would venture £100. upon a literary speculation he had in hand.

September 1 My Sheridan task in the morning: interrupted by Bowles[1], who never comes amiss; the mixture of talent and simplicity in him delightful. His parsonage-house at Brenhill is beautifully situated; but he has a good deal frittered away its beauty with grottoes, hermitages, and Shenstonian inscriptions: when company is coming he cries, "Here, John, run with the crucifix and missal to the hermitage, and set the fountain going." His sheep bells are tuned in thirds and fifths; but he is an excellent fellow notwithstanding; and, if the waters of his inspiration be not those of Helicon, they are at

[1] Rev. William Bowles, 1762–1850. Poet and antiquary. His sonnets, published in 1789, greatly influenced Coleridge and marked the change in poetical taste. The preface to his *Life of Pope* (1807) drew Byron, Campbell and others into a long and very spirited controversy.

least very *sweet* waters, and to my taste pleasanter than some that are more strongly impregnated.

October 3 Sheridan, the first time he met Tom, after the marriage of the latter, seriously angry with him; told him he had made his will, and had cut him off with a shilling. Tom said he was, indeed, very sorry, and immediately added, "You don't happen to have the shilling about you now, sir, do you?" Old S. burst out laughing, and they became friends again. The day that Dog Dent was to bring forward the motion (that gave him that name) about a tax upon dogs, S. came early to the house, and saw no one but Dent sitting in a contemplative posture in one corner. S. stole round to him unobserved, and putting his hand under the seat to Dent's legs, mimicked the barking of a dog, at which Dent started up alarmed, as if his conscience really dreaded some attack from the race he was plotting against. Sheridan angry with his servant for lighting a fire in a little room off his hall, because it tempted the duns to stay, by making them so comfortable. Mrs Sheridan wrote an entertainment called the "Haunted Village," which she gave S. to add some touches to, but never could get from him again. Linley seemed to think he suppressed it from jealousy. Leeves, a clergyman, was the author of the words of "Auld Robin Gray": I already knew Lady Anne Lindsay composed the music. Morel wrote some of the sweetest words in Handel's oratorio—"Tears such as tender fathers shed," &c. &c.; very sweet English this "for *joy* to think." We read to-night passages out of *Lewesdon Hill*; some of them of the highest order. Parr, when asked by Madame Madalina Palmer, how he liked Crowe, said, "Madam, I love him; he is the very brandy of genius, mixed with the stinking water of absurdity." To-day Bowles showed me a part of his library, in which was collected, he told me, all the books illustrative of the divines of the times of Charles I, and the theology of that period. The first book I put my hand on in this sacred corner was a volume of Tom Brown's works, &c. Bowles was amused in the midst of all his gravity by this detection. What with his genius, his blunders, his absences, &c., he is the most delightful of all existing parsons or poets. In talking of Miss Gayton, the pretty little dancer, marrying Murray, a clergyman, Joy applied two lines well, saying they might now, in their different capacities

> Teach men for heaven or money's sake,
> What *steps* they were through life to take.

October 7 The company at Bowood, besides those there on Sunday, the Hollands[1], Allen, Marsh, Henry Fox, Wellesley; and Charles Fox and Fazakerly arrived in the evening. Sat near Lady Holland at dinner; very gracious; has really shown a sincere anxiety about my Bermuda misfortune. They talked much about Brougham's "Letter on the Public Charities"; all seemed to condemn his strictures upon Eton and Winchester: an

[1] Lord and Lady Holland. Lord Holland (1773-1840) was the nephew of Charles James Fox and a fervent Whig; but his actual political career was insignificant compared with the part he played as a patron of literature. Lady Holland (1770-1845) was the most famous hostess of her time, and her dinner-table was the centre of Whig political and literary world.

answer to it coming out, got up by the Government, in a letter to Sir William Scott. Talked of poor Monk Lewis: his death was occasioned by taking emetics for sea-sickness, in spite of the advice of those about him. He died lying on the deck. When he was told all hope was over, he sent his man down below for pen, ink, and paper; asked him to lend him his hat; and upon that, as he lay, wrote a codicil to his will. Few men, once so talked of, have ever produced so little sensation by their death. He was ruining his Negroes in Jamaica, they say, by indulgence, for which they suffered severely as soon as his back was turned; but he has enjoined it to his heirs, as one of the conditions of holding his estate, that the Negroes were to have three additional holidays in the year; and has left a sort of programme of the way those holidays are to be celebrated—the hour when the overseer is to sound his shell to summon them together, the toasts, &c.: the first toast to be "the Lady Frederica, Duchess of York"; so like poor Lewis. Had a good deal of conversation with Lord Holland in the evening about Sheridan. Told me that one remarkable characteristic of S., and which accounted for many of his inconsistencies, was the high, ideal system he had formed of a sort of impracticable perfection in honour, virtue, &c., anything short of which he seemed to think not worth aiming at; and thus consoled himself for the extreme laxity of his practice by the impossibility of satisfying or coming up to the sublime theory he had formed. Hence the most romantic professions of honour and independence were coupled with conduct of the meanest and most swindling kind; hence, too, prudery and morality were always on his lips, while his actions were one series of debauchery and libertinism. A proof of this mixture was, after the Prince became Regent, he offered to bring S. into parliament, and said, at the same time, that he by no means meant to fetter him in his political conduct by doing so; but S. refused, because, as he told Lord Holland, "he had no idea of risking the high independence of character which he had always sustained, by putting it in the power of any man, by any possibility whatever, to dictate to him." Yet, in the very same conversation in which he paraded all this fine flourish of high-mindedness, he told Lord H. of an intrigue he had set on foot for inducing the Prince to lend him £4000. to purchase a borough. From his habit of considering money as nothing, he considered his *owing* the Prince £4000. as no slavery whatever: "I shall then (he said) *only* owe him £4000. which will leave me as free as air."—Sheridan's high opinion of his own powers of management, which made him often stand aloof from his party and friends. He was the means, said Lord H., of bringing Sidmouth in with us in 1806, and of bringing Ellenborough into the Cabinet. He was also the primary cause of the defection of the Prince from the Whigs, when he became Regent. On that event taking place, the Prince wrote to Lords Grey and Grenville to take measures for forming an administration. Their answer was shown by the Prince to Sheridan, who pointed out some things in it he thought objectionable. The Prince represented these to the two lords, who very imprudently returned a high-toned remonstrance to him for having shown their answer to S.

The latter was nettled, and, with equal imprudence, made such comments on the sort of tyranny to which these lords seemed already to aspire over the Prince, and let out so many other opinions with respect to them, that his Royal Highness became alarmed, and threw himself into the arms of the Tories. "These," said Lord Holland, "are secrets of too *cabinet* a nature, and too recent to be made use of by you." I said I believed that not only S., but Lord Moira, had never forgiven Lords G. and G. for the way in which they themselves (and, in their person, the Prince) were, as they thought, treated by them after the death of Mr Fox. I remember Lord Moira saying, "They actually pushed us from our stools; never consulted us about anything." Mentioned this. "I cannot think what he meant by that," said Lord Holland, "Moira is certainly the oddest mixture of *romance* and the reverse that ever existed. As to not consulting him, he always sat silent, and did not seem to attend to anything. As to our making no report to the Prince of what we were doing, we looked upon Moira as his organ there, and thought it would be officious of any one else to be the medium of communication." The fact is, Lord M.'s silence was evidently from pique at thinking himself neglected, and the only communication, of course, he made to the Prince was, to tell him that they never troubled their heads about him. All this accounts most satisfactorily for the defection of the Regent; and if anything could justify his duplicity and apostasy, it would be their arrogance and folly. Sheridan was jealous of Mr Fox, and showed it in ways that produced, at last, great coolness between them. He envied him particularly his being member for Westminster, and, in 1802, had nearly persuaded him to retire from parliament, in order that he might himself succeed to that honour. But it was Burke chiefly that S. hated and envied. Being both Irishmen, both adventurers, they had every possible incentive to envy. On Hastings' trial particularly it went to Sheridan's heart to see Burke in the place set apart for privy councillors, and himself excluded. This was all very amusing, and I was rather sorry I had arranged to return home at night. Everybody pressed me to stay, and I was very near having reason to repent my going; for, when we were about a mile from the house, Joy's coachman drove off the road down a bank, and overset the carriage. The crash was tremendous, for three of the glasses were up; but none of us were hurt, except Joy's man a little bruised in the hip, and my arm slightly strained. Lord Lansdowne's keeper happened luckily to be passing, and helped us to raise the carriage. I walked home, and did not arrive till past one o'clock.

In speaking of Sheridan's eloquence, Lord H. said that the over-strained notions he had of perfection were very favourable to his style of oratory in giving it a certain elevation of tone and dignity of thought. Mr Fox thought his Westminster Hall speech, trumpery, and used to say it spoiled the style of Burke, who was delighted with it. Certainly in the report I have read of it, it seems most trashy bombast.

October 9 Received a long letter from Lord Byron, in which he sends me two stanzas of the Beppo-ish poem he is about, called *Don Juan*. In the evening read Colman's little comedy of *Ways and Means* to Bessy[1] and Mary D. Some comical things in it: "Curse Cupid, he has not a halfpenny to buy breeches:" "Always threatening to break my neck; one would think we servants had a neck to spare, like the Swan in Lad Lane." Read some of S.'s speeches.

October 18 As the morning was fine, set out to Bowood to see Rogers[2]; caught him in the garden, on the way to Bowles's; walked with him; talked much about Sheridan. Sheridan once told Rogers of a scene that occurred in a French theatre in 1772, where two French officers stared a good deal at his wife, and S., not knowing a word of French, could do nothing but put his arms a-kimbo and look bluff and defying at them, which they, not knowing a word of English, could only reply to by the very same attitude and look. He once mentioned to Rogers that he was aware he ought to have made a love scene between Charles and Maria in the *School for Scandal*; and *would* have done it, but that the actors who played the parts were not able to do such a scene justice. Talked of Hastings and the impeachment. Asked Rogers whether it was not now looked upon, even by the Opposition themselves, as a sort of dramatic piece of display, got up by the Whigs of that day from private pique, vanity, &c. &c.;

---

[1] Elizabeth Moore, the poet's wife.
[2] Samuel Rogers (1763–1855). Poet and wealthy banker. He had a bitter tongue but was a good friend to less fortunate men of letters and had a real affection for Moore.

Francis, first urging them on from his hostility to Hastings; Burke running headlong into it from impetuosity of temper; and Sheridan seizing with avidity the first great opportunity that offered of showing off his talent. He said it *was* so considered now; and in addition to all this, Mr Pitt gave in to the prosecution with much satisfaction, because it turned away the embattled talent of the time from himself and his measures, and concentrated it all against this one individual, whom he was most happy to sacrifice, so he could thereby keep them employed. Burke's admiration of S.'s second speech on the Begums; said, "That is the true style; something neither prose nor poetry, but better than either." It was the opinion of Mr Fox that Burke's style altered after he heard this speech; that it spoiled him, and that to the taste he acquired from it we owe the extreme floridness of his writings afterwards—the passage about the Queen of France, &c. &c. Lord Holland had told me this before; but there seems to me but little in it. It was natural for the Whigs to think Burke's style much altered for the worse, when he wrote on the other side. Remarked to R. the forced and extravagant combinations by which S. so often laboured to produce effect both in his serious and his comic. The description of Bonaparte an instance: "Kings his sentinels, kingdoms his martello-towers, *crowns* and *sceptres* his pallisadoes," &c. Talked of the letter from Dr Chalmers to Lord Byron in the *Scot's Magazine*: in mentioning the great publicity Byron has given to his private sorrows, he says "you have *wailed on the house-top.*" This is excellent. Showed me Crowe's verses written for the installation of the Duke of Portland; never saw them before; noble poetry! Found Bowles at home; wants to have a statue of Melanchthon executed from the fine woodcut, to put up in his projected library; anxious to consult me about some prose he is writing. Left Bowles's at half-past two. In passing through Bowood for home I was caught by Lady Lansdowne, Lord Auckland, &c. &c. She begged me to stay for dinner; said Lady Bath (who was going next day) wished very much to know me. Party at dinner—Lady Bath, her unmarried daughter, Lady Louisa, and the married one, Lady Elizabeth Campbell and her husband; Lord Auckland and his two sisters; Mrs Frankland Lewis. Miss Eden's name Dulcibella. Talked of strange names: I mentioned a little child, born in Italy of English parents, christened Allegra. (*N.B.* a natural child of Lord Byron's, mentioned in his last letter to me.) Some traveller in America mentions having met a man called Romulus Riggs: whether true or not, very like their mixture of the classical and the low. Talked of the alterations at the late Dublin city dinners; about the toast of the "Glorious Memory"; mentioned that about the middle of the last century the usual adjunct to this toast was, "and a fig for the Bishop of Cork"; the Bishop, who was a strong Tory, having written a book against drinking Memories, pronouncing it to be idolatrous, &c. &c. Burke's bad manner of speaking, and the effect it had in quite nullifying the effect of his speeches. F. Lewis said he had heard Lord Grenville mention that once, after a speech of Burke's, himself and Pitt consulted with each other whether it was worth answering, and decided in the negative; *since*, however, it is one of the speeches that Lord Grenville said he had always read with most admiration and delight. I think it was upon the Nabob of Arcot's debts. Rogers asked me whether the *Parody on Horace*, lately in the *Chronicle*, was mine; said how Luttrell[1] was delighted with it at Ampthill, and pronounced it to be mine; reading it out to Lords Jersey and Duncannon, who were also much pleased with it. Told me also that he heard the verses to Sir Hudson Lowe praised at Brookes's. It is pleasant to find that these trifles do not die unnoticed. Lord Lansdowne[2] asked me afterwards, whether it was I who wrote a description of a dinner at the French Minister's (I think) about two months ago, which was, he said, most admirable. Told him *not*, nor had I ever seen it. He said he *knew* the *Parody on Horace* to be mine. Told him I had asked the Hollands whether what Trotter says of Mr Fox's refusal to see Sheridan in his last illness was true or not, and they answered it was true. Lord L. said he believed it to be so; and that his own opinion of Sheridan, which was very low indeed, had been formed principally

---

[1] Henry Luttrell (*c*. 1765–1851), illegitimate son of the Earl of Carhampton. He wrote light verse, and was a famous wit and diner-out, and was a friend of Moore's. His name recurs very frequently in the Journal.

[2] Henry Petty FitzMaurice, third marquess of Lansdowne (1780–1863). A leader of the Whig Party, Chancellor of the Exchequer at the age of twenty-six, and afterwards Secretary of State for home affairs, and Lord President of the Council. He and his wife, as will be seen, were among Moore's greatest friends.

from what he had heard Mr Fox say of him. Meant to walk home, but Lady L. insisted upon my having the coachman to drive me over in her little gig. Cannot sleep out while dear Bessy is so near her difficulties, and without a single male or female friend near her but myself. The Lansdownes very kind to me. I did *him* injustice in thinking that he had forgot my Bermuda calamity, for it was he who, in a letter to Ampthill, while I was last in town, mentioned that he feared it wore a darker aspect than it did before. Got home rather late.

October 19 Had promised Rogers, who was coming to me this morning, to meet him half way. Mrs Phipps, upon whom I called as I went, came out with me in order to get a glimpse of "*Memory* Rogers." He and I walked to my cottage; much delighted with the scenery around; said he preferred the valley and village before us to the laid-out grounds of Bowood. Showed him some of my Sheridan papers. He mentioned "Memoirs of Jackson" of Exeter, written by himself, which he saw in MS. some years ago, and in which he remembered there was a most glowing description of his pupil, Miss Linley, standing singing by his side, and so beautiful that "you might think you were looking into the face of an angel." I wish I had these "Memoirs." Walked with him to the village, and then as far as Phipps's, where I was to dine, in order to go to the Devizes ball in the evening. The ball dull enough; got home between two and three, and found Bess just rising from her bed to blow the fire for some hot drink for me.

October 21 Walked to meet Rogers, who said he would call upon me. Talked chiefly of Sheridan. Told me several anecdotes, some of which I have written down in my notebook as fit to use; the rest practical jokes, not easily tellable:—His strewing the hall or passage with plates and dishes, and knives and forks stuck between them, and then tempting Tickell (with whom he was always at some frolic or other) to pursue him into the thick of them: Tickell fell among them and was almost cut to pieces, and next day, in vowing vengeance to Lord John Townshend against S. for this trick, he added (with the true spirit of an amateur in practical jokes), "but it was amazingly well done." Another time, when the women (Mrs Crewe, Mrs Tickell, &c.) had received the gentlemen after dinner in disguises, which puzzled them to make out *which* was *which*, the gentlemen one day sent to the ladies to come downstairs to *them* in the dining-room. The ladies, upon entering, saw them all dressed as Turks, holding bumpers in their hands, and after looking amongst them and saying, "This is Mr Crewe;" "No, this is he," &c. &c. they heard a laugh at the door, and there they saw all the gentlemen *in propriis personis;* for 'twas the maids they had dressed up in Turkish habits. S. was always at these tricks in country houses...

...Talked of Beckford's two *mock* novels *Agemia* and the *Elegant Enthusiast*, which he wrote to ridicule the novels written by his sister, Mrs Harvey (I think), who read these parodies on herself quite innocently, and only now and then suspecting that they were meant to laugh at her, saying, "Why, I vow and protest, here is my grotto," &c. &c. In the *Elegant Enthusiast* the heroine writes a song which she sings at a masquerade, and which produces such an effect, that my Lord Mahogany, in the character of a Milestone, bursts into tears. It is in *Agemia* that all the heroes and heroines are killed at the conclusion by a supper of stewed lampreys.

October 22 Walked at twelve o'clock towards Bowood to meet Rogers.... Talked of the Scotch novels. When Wilkie the painter was taking his portrait's of Scott's family, the eldest daughter said to him, "We don't know what we think of those novels. We have access to all papa's papers. He has no particular study; writes everything in the midst of us all; and yet we never have seen a single scrap of the MS. of any of these novels; but still we have *one* reason for thinking them his, and that is, that they are the only works published in Scotland of which copies are not presented to papa." The reason *against* is stronger than the reason *for*: Scott gave his honour to the Prince Regent they were not his; and Rogers *heard* him do the same to Sheridan, who asked him, with some degree of *brusquerie*, whether he was the author of them. All this rather confirms me in my first idea that they are *not* Scott's. Another argument between us, on the justifiableness of a man asserting so solemnly that a book was *not his* when it really *was*; I maintained that no man had a right to put himself into a situation which required lies to support him in it.

October 23 ... Returned home to dinner at four; went to bed early, and was called up by Bessy at half-past eleven o'clock: sent for the mid-wife, who arrived between one and two, and at a quarter before four my darling Bessy was safely delivered of a son (and heir *in partibus*), to my unspeakable delight, for never had I felt half such anxiety about her. I walked about the parlour by myself, like one distracted; sometimes stopping to pray, sometimes opening the door to listen; and never was gratitude more fervent than that with which I knelt down to thank God for the dear girl's safety, when all was over—(the maid, by the by, very near catching me on my knees). Went to bed at six o'clock.

November 15 (*Sunday*) This day my own excellent Bessy has completed her twenty-fifth year[1]: she is much better this morning. Heaven send her many happy returns of this anniversary! Began another slang epistle. Finished *Joseph Andrews* to Bessy in the evening.

November 16 Went on with another slang epistle. Shall return to "Sheridan" with more pleasure after this change of key. Read the *Vicar of Wakefield* to Bessy in the evening. What a gem it is! we both enjoyed it so much more than *Joseph Andrews*. A man had come in the morning, a young Irishman, and said his wife had been delivered of twins on the road, and was lying without any comforts for them at a house in Sandy Lane: never could he have found Bessy in a tenderer

[1] Mrs Moore was born in 1793.

mood for such a story. She had a large jug of caudle made instantly, which she gave him, with two little caps and two shifts out of the stock she keeps for the poor, a pound of sugar, some tea, and two shillings; one of which was *my* gift, because he was an Irishman.

November 17 Our Irish friend did not bring back the pitcher as he promised. Suspicions began to arise; walked to Phipps's; called at the cottage where the fellow said his wife and twins were lying; found 'twas all a cheat. Sad hardeners of the heart these tricks are........Read the *Vicar of Wakefield* to Bessy in the evening.

November 18 Walked my dear Bessy for the first time into the garden; the day delightful. She went round to all her flower beds to examine their state, for she had every little leaf in the garden by heart. Took a ramble afterwards by myself through the Valley of Chitoway, and the fields. Exactly such a day as that described so beautifully by the sacred poet Herbert:

> Sweet day, so cool, so calm, so bright,
> The bridal of the earth and sky;
> Sweet dews shall weep thy fall to-night
> For thou must die.

In the evening, finished the *Vicar of Wakefield* to Bessy; we both cried over it. Returned thanks to God most heartily for the recovery of my darling girl, and slept soundly.

November 26 Went to Holland House; had some conversation with Lord H. before dinner. Mentioned to me a curious scene which he had with Sheridan and the Prince while they were in power. S. having told him (while they waited in an ante-chamber) about some public letter which he had corrected or re-written for the Prince, the latter, on their admission to him, told quite a different story, referring to S., who all the while courteously bowed assent; and, said Lord H., "I could not, for the soul of me, make out which was the liar."

November 29 ... Dined to-day with Scrope Davies to meet Jackson the boxer at my own request, as I want to pick up as much of the flash, *from authority*, as possible. Some talk with Davies before dinner, about Lord Byron and me having been so near blowing each other's brains out: told him that Lord B. had said since he never meant to fire at me. Davies was with him at the time this hostile correspondence took place, and offered to bet upon friendship against fighting as the most likely result. The event found him right. Lord B's conduct on this occasion was full of manliness and candour. Got very little out of Jackson; he makes, Davies tells me, more than a thousand a year by teaching sparring.

December 1 Called upon Gifford, editor of the *Quarterly*; have known him long, but forbore from calling upon him ever since I meditated *Lalla Rookh*, lest it might look like trying to propitiate his criticism; the mildest man in the world till he takes a pen in his hand, but then all gall and spitefulness.

December 2 Conversation at breakfast about late hours. The porter of the late Lord Jersey came to some one and complained he could not stay with the Jerseys, "because my lady was the very latest woman in London." "Well, but what then? All women of fashion are late, you can sleep afterwards." "Ah no, sir, that's not all, for my Lord is the earliest gentleman in London; and, between the two, I get no sleep at all." I mentioned the circumstance of a man from the country visiting his friend in town, and both sleeping in the same bed, without ever meeting for a fortnight.

December 4 Breakfasted with Davies at seven. Walked to Jackson's house in Grosvenor Street; a very neat establishment for a boxer. Were off in our chaise at eight. The immense crowds of carriages, pedestrians, &c., all along the road—the respect paid to Jackson everywhere, highly comical. He sung some flash songs on the way, and I contrived to muster up one or two myself, much to Scrope Davies's surprise and diversion. The scene of action beyond Crawley, thirty-two miles from town; the combatants Randall and Turner, the former an Irishman, which was lucky, as it gave me some sort of interest in the contest. The thing altogether not so horrid as I expected. Turner's face was a good deal de-humanised, but Randall (the conqueror) had hardly a scratch. The battle lasted two hours and twenty-two minutes: a beautiful sunshine broke out at this part of the day; and had there been a proportionate mixture of women in the immense ring formed around, it would have been a very brilliant spectacle. The pigeons let off at different periods of the fight, with despatches, very picturesque; at the close, as many as half a dozen took wing. It seems they are always sure messengers, unless they happen to meet with a hawk.

December 6 Breakfasted at Rogers's. Told me of Crabbe's negotiation with Murray for his new volume of "Tales," consisting of near 12,000 lines. Murray offered him for this and the copyright of the past volumes £3000. Crabbe was at breakfast with us, and seemed to think this was a good bargain; and so, I confess, did I; but Rogers thought this sum should be given for the new volume alone, and that the Longmans ought to be tried. Went to Longmans; settled some more of business; from thence to Wilkie, who produced me two large bags of Sheridan's papers to examine. Worked at them for two hours. By the by, much talk in town about "Brummel's Memoirs." Murray told me a day or two ago, that the report was he had offered £5000. for the "Memoirs," but that the Regent had sent Brummel £6000. to suppress them! Upon Murray's saying he really had some idea of going to Calais to treat with Brummel, I asked him (Scrope Davies was by) what he would give me for a volume in the style of the "Fudges," on his correspondence and interviews with Brummel? "A thousand guineas," he said, "this instant." But I rather think I should be tempted to quiz Master Murray, in such a work, a little more than he would like.

December 23 Read the *Heart of Mid-Lothian* to Bessy in the evening. Have got a wet-nurse for little Tommy, a woman in the neighbourhood, to come three times a day, which is better than nothing. Poor little thing! with a mother that can give him no milk, and a father that can give him no money, what business has he in this world! Bowles had called in the morning; and was most amusing about his purchase of a great coat once in Monmouth Street, which while in the shop he took for blue, but which on his appearance in the sunshine he found to be a glaring glossy green. His being met in this coat by a great church dignitary, &c. &c.

December 30 Routed out of my study by the preparations for the dance to-morrow night, and not able to get into my *other* study, the garden, on account of the damp, foggy weather. Copied out some music. At a quarter to six, Macdonald called upon me to go to dinner at Bowood; obliged to feel our way, not very safely, through the fog....

...Sir J. Mackintosh[1] told of "Barry Close," the well-known East Indian officer, that not having learned anything previous to his going to India, he got everything he knew through the medium of *Persian* literature; studied logic in a translation (from Arabic into Persian) of Aristotle; and was a most learned and troublesome *practician*, as well, as theorist, in dialectics. Some one brought him a volume of Lord Bacon (of whom he had never heard) and said, "Here is a man who has attacked your friend, Aristotle, tooth and nail." "Who can the impudent fellow be?" said Close. "Lord Bacon." "Who

[1] Sir James Mackintosh (1765-1832), historian and jurist, who made a famous reply to Burke's *Reflections on the French Revolution*. He was one of the most brilliant members of the Holland House circle and was renowned as an encyclopædic talker.

the devil is he? What trash people do publish in these times!" After reading him, however, he confessed that Lord Bacon had said some devilish sensible things. Music in the evening; all but Mackintosh and the elder Macdonald attentive. They talked the whole time: I did not mind Macdonald; but I was sorry for Mackintosh. I said, when I got up from singing, "I see those two gentlemen like to talk to accompaniment," which brought the rest of the company upon them, and they were put to the blush.

December 31 All bustle and preparation for our dance in the evening; the supper laid in my study. Poor Bessy on her legs all day, to get everything as nice as possible; my chief occupation, besides drawing the wine, to keep little Tom quiet. All went off most gaily. We did our best to make them happy; and, to do our guests justice, they seemed all to come with a determination to be pleased. Supped at half-past twelve. I had lobsters, oysters, and champagne, express from London for the occasion, and the supper looked not only gay but elegant. Twenty-two persons supped in my little study. I sang for them after supper, and then to dancing again till near four in the morning. Poor Bessy's eyes, which have been sore for some days, dreadfully inflamed and red through the whole evening. A gay beginning to the new year.

January 28 Went to breakfast with Rogers, who is in the very agonies of parturition: showed me the work ready printed and in boards, but he is still making alterations: told me that Lord Byron's *Don Juan* is pronounced by Hobhouse and others as unfit for publication. Crabbe's delight at having three thousand pounds in his pocket. R. offered to take care of the bills for him, but no, he must take them down to show them to his son John. "Would not copies do?" "No, must show son John the actual notes."

January 31 Went to breakfast with Hobhouse[1], in order to read Lord Byron's poem: a strange production, full of talent and singularity, as everything he writes must be: some highly beautiful passages, and some highly humorous ones; but, as a whole, not publishable. Don Juan's mother is Lady Byron, and not only her learning, but various other points about her, ridiculed. He talks of her favourite dress being dimity (which is the case), dimity rhyming very comically with sublimity; and the conclusion of one stanza is, "I hate a dumpy woman," meaning Lady B. again. This would disgust the public beyond endurance. There is also a systemised profligacy running through it, which would not be borne. Hobhouse has undertaken the delicate task of letting him know our joint opinions.

March 20 [AT BATH] Called upon Lady C. Fitzgerald at half-past eleven. She mentioned that young D'Arblay (Miss Burney's son) had all *Lalla Rookh* by heart: praised him highly. Returned in an hour to Bowles, who wished me to read what he had done in answer

---

[1] John Cam Hobhouse, afterwards Baron Broughton (1786–1869), politician and the friend of Byron, with whom he travelled in 1809 and later. He wrote some notes for *Childe Harold*.

to Campbell. Found him in the bar of the White Hart, dictating to a waiter (who acted as amanuensis for him) his ideas of the true sublime in poetry: never was there such a Parson Adams since the real one.

April 1 Made Bessy turn her cap awry in honour of the day.

April 18 Took my little bible to church with me, in order to search in it for a subject that would suit a fine triumphant air of Novello's I have to put words to. Found an admirable one in Jeremiah, and wrote four lines during service—War against Babylon: much better employed than I should have been in listening to the drawling parson and snuffling clerk. Let nobody see me though, having the pew to myself and the two little girls.

May 13 Bessy and the little ones arrived: gave them up my lodgings, and took a bed at Rogers's. Went to Miller's Wharf, to secure berths for them in the packet for Sunday. The price of a state cabin seven guineas; but did not feel comfortable at the idea of their being all cribbed up in such a narrow space, and indulged in the extravagance of giving fourteen guineas for two cabins. Returned home at four: took a hackney-coach, and went with Bessy to Hornsey to visit the grave of our dearest Barbara. Her feelings seem to grow more quiet and reconciled on this subject. At eight o'clock she and I sauntered up and down the Burlington Arcade: then went and bought some prawns, and supped most snugly together.

May 19 Dined at Holland House. Company: Lord Grey, Lord A. Hamilton, Mrs Fox, Miss Fox, Sir J. Mackintosh, Tierney, &c. Their mixture of the doleful and the humorous in their discourse upon last night's defeat in the House of Commons very amusing. The censer flung round the room by Lady H.'s page after dinner seemed to astonish Murray the advocate, who had not, I suppose, seen the ceremony before; and I was myself a little astonished on hearing, as I came away, a very good male voice singing to the guitar, and finding that it was the *butler* who was accompanying himself in an Italian air. By the by the incense burned after dinner here comes from a convent in Spain, which gets it from another establishment connected with it in the north of Persia.

October 7 (IN ITALY) Did not leave Vicenza till seven; arrived at Padua about ten; took a *servitore di piazza* and went to see the churches, &c. Left Padua at twelve, and arrived at Lord Byron's country house, La Mira, near Fusina, at two. He was but just up and in his bath; soon came down to me; first time we have met these five years; grown fat, which spoils the picturesqueness of his head. The Countess Guiccioli, whom he followed to Ravenna, came from thence with him to Venice by the consent, it appears, of her husband. Found him in high spirits and full of his usual frolicksome gaiety. He insisted upon my making use of his house at Venice while I stay, but could not himself leave the Guiccioli. He drest, and we set off together in my carriage for Venice; a glorious sunset when we embarked at Fusina in a gondola, and the view of Venice and the distant Alps (some of which had snow on them, reddening with the last light) was magnificent; but my companion's conversation, which, though highly ludicrous and amusing, was anything but romantic, threw my mind and imagination into a mood not at all agreeing with the scene. Arrived at his palazzo on the Grand Canal (he having first made the gondolier row round in order to give me a sight of the Piazetta), where he gave orders with the utmost anxiety and good nature for my accommodation, and despatched persons in search of a *laquais de place* and his friend Mr Scott, to give me in charge to. No opera this evening. He ordered dinner from a traiteur's, and stopped to dine with me. Had much curious conversation with him about his wife before Scott arrived. He has written his memoirs, and is continuing them; thinks of going and purchasing lands under the Patriotic Government in South America. Much talk about *Don Juan*; he is writing a third canto; the Duke of Wellington; his taking so much money; gives instances of disinterested men, Epaminondas, &c. &c. down to Pitt himself, who,

> As minister of state, is
> Renown'd for ruining Great Britain gratis.

At nine o'clock he set off to return to La Mira, and I went with Mr Scott to two theatres; at the first a comedy, *Il prigionero de Newgate*, translated from the French; at the second, a tragedy of Alfieri, *Ottavia*; actors all disagreeable. Forgot to mention that Byron introduced me to his Countess before we left La Mira:

she is a blonde and young; married only about a year, but not very pretty.

October 8 ... Lord B. came up to town at six o'clock, and he and I dined with Scott at the Pellegrino: showed us a letter which his Countess had just received from her husband, in which, without a word of allusion to the way in which she is living with B., he makes some proposal with respect to money of B.'s being invested in his hands, as a thing advantageous to both; a fine specimen of an Italian husband.

May 28; *June* [IN PARIS] Here follows an interval of near a month, during which I have taken "no note of time," on account of the various distractions that have occupied every minute; among which, the chief was the finishing my work for the Longmans.... Received a letter from Lord Byron about the 7th or 8th, commissioning me to find out an Irishwoman of the name of M——, who had written to him to request he would let her have the proof sheets of one of his new works that she might translate it into French, and so make a little money by being first in the field with a translation, she being an orphan, &c. He begged me, if I found she was deserving of assistance, to draw upon him for a few hundred francs for her; but to tell her, "not to translate him, as that would be the height of ingratitude." She had said in her letter to him, "Moore is here, and is writing; I might ask *him*, but it is a Life of Johnson; and the French don't care about Johnson." I called upon the lady, and found her so respectably dressed and lodged, that I felt delicate, at first, about mentioning the gift Lord Byron intended for her; and when, on my second visit, I presented the fifteen Napoleons, the poor girl refused them, saying it was not in that way she wished to be served; having contrived hitherto, though an orphan, to support herself without pecuniary assistance from any one. She began to talk about "Moore"; upon which I thought it right to declare who I was; and her broad Irish stare at the communication was not a little diverting.

September 9 [IN PARIS] Kenny[1] told me that John Lamb (the brother of Charles), once knocked down Hazlitt who was impertinent to him, and on those who were present interfering, and begging of Hazlitt to shake hands and forgive him, H. said, "Well I don't care if I do. I am a metaphysician, and do not mind a blow; nothing but an *idea* hurts *me*."

October 24 [IN PARIS] Went with Bessy to market, and afterwards called upon Wordsworth. A young Frenchman called in, and it was amusing to hear him and Wordsworth at cross purposes upon the subject of *Athalie*; Wordsworth saying that he did not wish to see it acted, as it would never come up to the high imagination he had formed in reading it, of the prophetic inspiration of the priests, &c. &c.; and the Frenchman insisting that in acting alone could it be properly enjoyed,—that is to say, in the manner it was acted *now*; for he acknowledged that until the Corps de Ballet came to its aid, it was very dull, even on the

[1] James Kenney (1780–1849), dramatist, a friend of Charles Lamb.

stage,—*une action morte*. Saw Wordsworth's wife; she seems a comfortable sort of person enough. A note came from Lady Mary while I was there, to offer us both seats in her box at the Français, for the evening; and the struggle of Wordsworth (who had already arranged to go with his wife and sister there) between nobility and domesticity was very amusing. After long hesitation, however, and having written one note to say he must attend his wife, *my Lady* carried it, and he wrote another accepting the seat. I should have liked well enough to have gone myself, but this was our dear little Tom's birthday, and I had promised to pass the evening at home. Walked with Wordsworth, who was going to call upon Canning, and finding that Canning expected him, by his having left his name and Peel's with the porter, did not go up. While I was at dinner, a note arrived from Canning to ask me to dinner tomorrow. This is excellent! Can he ever have read the verses in the later editions of the *Fudge Family*? I fear not. Wrote to say I should have the honour of waiting on him.

October 25 [IN PARIS] Dined with Canning. Company: Lord and Lady Frederick Bentinck, Wordsworth, and the secretary, young Chinnery. The day very agreeable. I felt myself excited in an unusual way, and talked (I sometimes feared) rather too much; but they seemed to like it, and to be amused. There was one circumstance which showed a very pleasant sort of intelligence between the father and daughter. I told a story to Miss Canning, which the father was the only one who overheard, and it evidently struck them both as very comical. Canning said some very pleasant things, and in a very quiet, unobtrusive manner. Talking of Grattan, he said that, for the last two years, his public exhibitions were a complete failure, and that you saw all the mechanism of his oratory without its life. It was like lifting the flap of a barrel-organ and seeing the wheels. That this was unlucky, as it proved what an artificial style he had used. You saw the skeleton of his sentences without the flesh on them; and were induced to think that what you had considered flashes, were merely primings, kept ready for the occasion. Wordsworth rather dull. I see he is a man to *hold forth*; one who does not understand the *give and take* of conversation.

October 27 [IN PARIS] Wordsworth came at half-past eight, and stopped to breakfast. Talked a good deal. Spoke of Byron's plagiarisms from him; the whole third canto of *Childe Harold* founded on his style and sentiments. The feeling of natural objects which is there expressed, not caught by B. from nature herself, but from him (Wordsworth), and spoiled in the transmission. *Tintern Abbey* the source of it all; from which same poem too the celebrated passage about Solitude, in the first canto of *Childe Harold*, is (he said) taken, with this difference, that what is naturally expressed by him, has been worked by Byron into a laboured and antithetical sort of declamation. Spoke of the Scottish novels. Is sure they are Scott's. The only doubt he ever had on the question did not arise from thinking them too good to be Scott's, but, on the contrary, from the infinite number of clumsy things in them; commonplace contrivances, worthy only of the Minerva press, and such bad vulgar English as no gentleman of education ought to have written. When I mentioned the abundance of them, as being rather too great for one man to produce, he said, that great fertility was the characteristic of all novelists and story-tellers. Richardson could have gone on for ever; his *Sir Charles Grandison* was, originally, in thirty volumes. Instanced Charlotte Smith, Madame Cottin, &c. &c. Scott, since he was a child, accustomed to legends, and to the exercise of the story-telling faculty; sees nothing to stop him as long as he can hold a pen. Spoke of the very little real knowledge of poetry that existed now; so few men had time to study. For instance, Mr Canning; one could hardly select a cleverer man; and yet, what did Mr Canning know of poetry? What time had he, in the busy political life he had led, to study Dante, Homer, &c. as they ought to be studied, in order to arrive at the true principles of taste in works of genius. Mr Fox, indeed, towards the latter part of his life, made leisure for himself, and took to improving his mind; and, accordingly, all his later public displays bore a greater stamp of wisdom and good taste than his early ones. Mr Burke alone was an exception to this description of public men; by far the greatest man of his age; not only abounding in knowledge himself, but feeding, in various directions, his most able contemporaries; assisting Adam Smith in his *Political Economy*, and Reynolds in his *Lectures on Painting*. Fox, too, who acknowledged that all he had ever learned from books was nothing

to what he had derived from Burke. I walked with
Wordsworth to the Tuileries: he goes off to-morrow.
Bessy and I called upon Lady Davy at half-past two,
and drove about with her till it was time to go to dinner
at Grignon's. Told me that Sir Humphrey has mentioned in a letter she has just received from him, that
he has at present some important discovery in his head;
bids her not breathe a word of it to any Frenchman;
and says, "the game I aim at is of the highest sort."
Another discovery, such as that of the lamp, is too much
to expect from one man. We talked of Wordsworth's
exceedingly high opinion of himself; and she mentioned
that one day, in a large party, Wordsworth, without
anything having been previously said that could lead to
the subject, called out suddenly from the top of the
table to the bottom, in his most epic tone, "Davy!"
and, on Davy's putting forth his head in awful expecta-
tion of what was coming, said, "Do you know the
reason why I published the *White Doe* in quarto?"
"No, what was it?" "To show the world my own
opinion of it."

November 18 [IN PARIS] Had a letter from the Longmans, to say that the hope they had of finding out from
my deputy that the money had never been paid into
his hands, had been disappointed, and they must now
proceed to negotiate as soon as possible. Kenny called
in, and speaking of such a calamity coming upon one
so perfectly innocent of all delinquency as I am, said,
"It is well you are a poet; a philosopher could never
have borne it." There is a great deal of truth as well as

humour in this. Kenny wrote his *Raising the Wind* in seven days.

November 20 Had a letter from Lord Byron; very amusing; several epigrams in it; one of them for the approaching anniversary of his marriage (2nd of next January), most marvellously comical:—

>   To Penelope
> This day of all our days has done
>   The worst for me and you;
> 'Tis now six years since we were *one*,
>   And five since we were *two*.

December 16 [IN PARIS] Dined (Bessy and I) at Lord Charlemont's; the dear girl looking all neatness and beauty; not so pretty as Lady Charlemont certainly, but having the advantage of more youth on her side. The day very agreeable. Lord John told us a good trick of Sheridan's upon Richardson. Sheridan had been driving out three or four hours in a hackney coach, when, seeing Richardson pass, he hailed him and made him get in. He instantly contrived to introduce a topic upon which Richardson (who was the very soul of disputatiousness) always differed with him; and at last, affecting to be mortified at R.'s arguments, said, "You really are too bad; I cannot bear to listen to such things; I will not stay in the same coach with you"; and accordingly got down and left him, Richardson hallooing out triumphantly after him, "Ah, you're beat, you're beat"; nor was it till the heat of his victory had a little cooled that he found out he was left in the lurch to pay for Sheridan's three hours' coaching.

March 5 Willoughby mentioned that Talleyrand once, upon somebody who squinted asking him, "Comment vont vos affaires," answered "Comme vous voyez."

March 25 This day ten years we were married, and, though Time has made his usual changes in us both, we are still more like lovers than any married couples of the same standing I am acquainted with. Asked to dine at Rancliffe's, but dined at home alone with Bessy. This being Sunday, our dance, in celebration of the day, deferred till to-morrow. Received a letter yesterday from my dear father, which, notwithstanding the increased tremor of his hand, is written with a clearness of head and warmth of heart that seemed to promise many years of enjoyment still before him. God grant it!

March 26 [IN PARIS] Bessy busy in preparations for the dance this evening. I went and wrote to my dear mother, and told her, in proof of the unabated anxiety and affection I feel towards her, that a day or two ago, on my asking Bessy, "whether she would be satisfied if little Tom loved her through life as well as I love my mother," she answered, "Yes, if he loves me but a quarter as much." Went into town too late to return to dinner, and dined at Véry's alone. Found on my return our little rooms laid out with great management, and decorated with quantities of flowers, which Mrs Story had sent. Our company, Mrs S. and her cousins, Mrs Forster, her two daughters, and Miss Bridgeman, the Villamils, Irving[1], Capt. Johnson, Wilder, &c., and the Douglases. Began with music; Mrs V., Miss Drew, and Emma Forster sang. Our dance afterwards to the pianoforte very gay, and not the less so for the floor giving way in sundry places: a circle of chalk was drawn round one hole. Dr Yonge was placed sentry over another, and whenever there was a new crash, the general laugh at the heavy foot that produced it caused more merriment than the solidest floor in Paris could have given birth to. Sandwiches, negus, and champagne crowned the night, and we did not separate till near four in the morning. Irving's humour began to break out as the floor broke in, and he was much more himself than ever I have seen him. Read this morning, before I went out, *Thérèse Aubert*, and cried over it like a girl.

April 13 [IN PARIS] Dined with Lord Trimlestown: company, Lord Granard, Lattin, Harry Bushe, &c. Lattin and I told Irish stories by the dozen. Some of his very amusing. A posting dialogue: "Why, this chaise is very damp," "And a very good right it has to be so, sir; wasn't it all night in the canal?" Found, on my return home at night, Lord Byron's letter about Bowles and Pope, which Fielding had sent me to look over. The whole thing unworthy of him; a leviathan among small fry.

April 15 [IN PARIS] Dined at Fielding's: George Dawson and Montgomery. Dawson told a good story

---

[1] Washington Irving (1783–1859), the American essayist and historian, who spent a great part of his life in Europe, and appears frequently in these memoirs.

about the Irish landlord counting out the change of a guinea. "Twelve, 13, 14" (a shot heard); "Bob, go and see who's that that's killed; 15, 16, 17"; (enter Bob) "It's Kelly, sir."—"Poor Captain Kelly, a very good customer of mine; 18, 19, 20, there's your change, sir."

May 3 [IN PARIS] Received this morning Lord Byron's tragedy. Looked again over his letter on Bowles. It is amusing to see through his design in thus depreciating all the present school of poetry. Being quite sure of his own hold upon fame, he contrives to loosen that of all his contemporaries, in order that they may fall away entirely from his side, and leave him unencumbered, even by their floundering. It is like that Methodist preacher who, after sending all his auditory to the devil, thus concluded,—"You may perhaps, on the day of judgment, think to escape by laying hold of my skirts as I go to heaven; but it won't do; I'll trick you all; for I'll wear a spencer, I'll wear a spencer." So Lord B. willingly surrenders the skirts of his poetical glory, rather than let any of us poor devils stick in them, even for ever so short a time. The best of it is, too, that the wise public all the while turns up its eyes, and exclaims, "How modest!"

May 21 [IN PARIS] This is the day I fixed with Madame de Broglie to meet M. de Lafayette at dinner; went in at two. Received two letters from Lord Byron. In one of them he says that the lines on the Neapolitans, which I sent him, "are sublime as well as beautiful, and in my very best mood and manner." Company at the Duc de Broglie's, Lord and Lady Bessborough, Duc and Duchesse Dalberg, Wm. Schlegel, Count Forbin, M. de Lafayette, Auguste de Staël, the Swedish Ambassador, and, to my surprise, Madame Durazzo, of whom I have been hearing so much in all directions. A fine woman; must have been beautiful; not at all like an Italian. Sat next Miss Randall, and had much talk about Lord Byron. She said Lord B. was much wronged by the world; that he took up wickedness as a *subject*, just as Chateaubriand did religion, without either of them having much of the reality of either feeling in their hearts. Had much talk with Schlegel in the evening, who appears to me full of literary coxcombry: spoke of Hazlitt, who, he said, *l'avoit depassé* in his critical opinions, and was an ultra-Shaksperian. Is evidently not well inclined towards Lord Byron; thinks he will outlive himself, and get out of date long before he dies. Asked me if I thought a regular critique of all Lord B.'s works, and the system on which they are written, would succeed in England, and seems inclined to undertake it. Found fault with the *Edinburgh* and *Quarterly* for not being sufficiently European (in other words, for not taking notice enough of M. Schlegel and his works). Auguste de Staël, in praising these works, said that if there came a being fresh from another planet, to whom he wished to give a clear and noble idea of the arts, literature, philosophy, &c. of this earth, he would present to him the *Edinburgh Review*. M. Schlegel seemed to think that this planetary visitant had much better come to *him* for information.

June 5 [IN PARIS] A large party asked to dine at Villamil's to-day. Begged of him to let the dinner take place at our cottage instead, as the alarming state of the child would make it uncomfortable for him to have company at his home; but he preferred letting it remain as it was. Company there: the Storys, the Sapios, Dr Williams, Wilder, Irving, Mr Hinchcliffe, and Kenny after dinner. Neither Bessy nor Mrs Villamil came down. Bessy resolved to sit up with little Mary to-night, who was evidently dying.

June 6 [IN PARIS] At about a quarter after ten this morning the poor little thing died. Bessy and Dr Williams sat up with it the whole night, and Bessy had it for six hours on her lap, where at last it died. Williams said he never saw anything like the strength of mind, and indeed, of body, which Bessy showed throughout the whole time. This day altogether very gloomy. We dined with Villamil, and he, and I, and Williams walked in the evening.

June 7 This day still more miserable than yesterday; the weather wretched, and the house comfortless and deserted, from Bessy being away all day with Mrs Villamil. Wrote a few lines.

June 13 [IN PARIS] Went in for the purpose of dining with the Hollands. Called on Lady Bessborough; told me that, when she was a child, she was *en pension* at Versailles; used to be a good deal taken notice of by Marie Antoinette; spoke of the very striking air of dignity her countenance could assume. On one occasion, when she (Lady B.) had been playing with her in the morning, there was to be a reception of ambassadors, whom it was the custom for the Queen to receive sitting at the bottom of the bed. The child, anxious to see the ceremony, hid herself in the bed-curtains, and was so astonished and even terrified by the change which took place in the Queen's countenance, on the entrance of the ambassadors, that the feeling has never been forgotten by her to this hour. Met Luttrell on the Boulevards and walked with him. In remarking a rather pretty woman who passed he said, "The French women are often in the suburbs of beauty, but never enter the town." Company at Lord Holland's, Allen, Henry Fox, the *black* Fox (attached to the Embassy), Denon, and, to my great delight, Lord John Russell[1], who arrived this morning. Lord Holland told before dinner (*à propos* of something), of a man who professed to have studied "Euclid" all through, and upon some one saying to him, "Well, solve me that problem," answered, "Oh, I never looked at the cuts." The dinner rather *triste* and *géné*, both from Lord Holland's absence (being laid up with the gout) and Denon's presence, *one* foreigner always playing the deuce with a dinner-party.

---

[1] Lord John Russell, afterwards Earl Russell (1792–1878), the Whig statesman prominently associated with Catholic Emancipation and Parliamentary Reform. He was a life-long friend of Moore's, and on the death of the latter, in 1852, acted as his literary executor and edited the *Memoirs, Journal and Correspondence of Thomas Moore*.

July 3 [IN PARIS] Company at the Holland's, Lambton, Lady Louisa and her sister, Lord Alvanley, Lord John, Lattin, Lord Thanet, Lord Gower, &c. Talking of Delille, Lord H. said that, notwithstanding his pretty description of Kensington Gardens, he walked with him once there, and he did not know them when he was in them. Mad. de Staël never looked at anything; passed by scenery of every kind without a glance at it; which did not, however, prevent her describing it. I said that Lord Byron could not describe anything which he had not had actually under his eyes, and that he did it either on the spot or immediately after. This, Lord Holland remarked, was the sign of a true poet, to write only from *impressions*; but where then do all the imaginary scenes of Dante, Milton, &c. go, if it is necessary to *see* what we describe in order to be a true poet?

July 6 [IN PARIS] Busy preparing the *pavillon* for Lord John. Our company to dinner: Lord Granard, Lady Adelaide, Lady Caroline, Lord John, Luttrell, Fazakerley, and Villamil. The day very agreeable. Luttrell in good spirits, and highly amusing: told of an Irishman, who, having jumped into the water to save a man from drowning, upon receiving sixpence from the person as a reward for the service, looked first at the sixpence, then at him, and at last exclaimed, "By Jasus, I'm *over*-paid for the job." Lord John told us that Bobus Smith one day, in conversation with Talleyrand, having brought in somehow the beauty of his mother, T. said "C'étoit donc votre père qui n'étoit pas bien." By the bye, I yesterday gave Lady Holland

Lord Byron's "Memoirs" to read; and on my telling her that I rather feared he had mentioned her name in an unfair manner somewhere, she said, "Such things give me no uneasiness: I know perfectly well my station in the world; and I know all that can be said of me. As long as the few friends that I *really* am sure of speak kindly of me (and I would not believe the contrary if I saw it in black and white), all that the rest of the world can say is a matter of complete indifference to me." There are some fine points about Lady Holland; she is a warm and active friend, and I should think her capable of *high-mindedness* upon occasions.

July 26 [IN PARIS] Dined at Lattin's; company, Lords Holland, John Russell, Thanet, and Trimlestown; Messrs. Maine de Biron and Denon, Luttrell, and Concannon. Abundance of noise and Irish stories from Lattin; some of them very good. A man asked another to come and dine off boiled beef and potatoes with him. "That I will," says the other; "and it's rather odd it should be exactly the same dinner I had at home for myself, *barring the beef*." ... In talking of the feeling of the Irish for Buonaparte, Lattin said, that when he was last in Ireland, he has been taken to a secret part of the cabin by one of his poor tenants, who whispered "I'll know *you'll* not betray me, sir: but just look there, and tell me whether that's the *real thing*," pointing to a soi-disant portrait of Buonaparte, which was neither more nor less than a print of Marshal Saxe, or some such ancient. Denon told an anecdote of a man, who having been asked repeatedly to dinner by a person

whom he knew to be but a shabby Amphitryon, went
at last, and found the dinner so meagre and bad, that
he did not get a bit to eat. When the dishes were
removing, the host said, "Well, now the ice is broken,
I suppose you will ask me to dine with you some day."—
"Most willingly." "Name your day, then."—"Aujourd'hui, par exemple," answered the dinnerless guest.
Lord Holland told of a man remarkable for absence,
who, dining once at the same sort of shabby repast,
fancied himself in his own house, and began to apologise
for the wretchedness of the dinner.

September 27 [IN LONDON] Power called, then Lord
John, and at last Murray. There was a mistake in the
delivery of my note to him yesterday, which caused
the delay. Agreed to all my arrangements about the
payment of the sum for the "Memoirs;" took away
the MS. Says that Lord B.'s two last tragedies
(*Sardanapalus* and *Foscari*) are worth nothing; that
nobody will read them. Offered Lord B. £1000. for
the continuation of *Don Juan*, and the same for the
two tragedies; which he refused. Advised Murray not
to speak so freely of his transactions with Lord B.,
nor of the decrease which, he says, has taken place in
the attraction of his works. *Don Juan* to be discontinued, at the request (as, according to him, Byron
says) of the Countess Guiccioli.

October 23 [IN LONDON] ...Called on Chantrey, who
seemed heartily glad to see me; his *atelier* full of mind;
never saw such a set of *thinking* heads as his busts.

Walter Scott's very remarkable from the height of the head. The eyes, Chantrey says, are usually taken as a centre, and the lower portion (or half) always much the greater; but in Scott's head the upper part is even longer than the lower. Explained to me in what cases the eyes ought to be marked or picked out, and in what not.

November 8 Sailed in the "Rob Roy" at half-past seven; wind and sea against us; five hours' passage. Arrived at half-past two; obliged to stay till to-morrow on account of the custom house. Met Brummell (the exile of Calais)[1], and had some conversation with him.

March 4 [IN PARIS] Received a letter from Lord Byron, who signs himself now *Noel Byron*. He has called out Southey[2], as I expected he would, and he has done right; no man should suffer such a letter as Southey's, signed with his name, to pass without this sort of notice. Lord B. ought not to have brought it upon himself, but, having done so, there was but this left for him. Neither will any harm result from it, as Southey, I am sure, will not meet him.

April 15 The scene of our departure (at about half-past four) very amusing; all the fashionable of Boulogne, in gigs, carriages, curricles, &c. on the pier. Resurrection of many Irish friends whom I had thought no

[1] The famous Beau Brummell, who ended his days at Calais.
[2] In consequence of a letter which appeared in the London *Courier*, Jan. 5, 1822, in reply to some strictures made by Lord Byron on Mr Southey's Preface to his *Vision of Judgment*. [Lord John Russell's Note.]

longer *above the world*: Tom Grady, who told me that there was some other region (unknown) to which those, who exploded at Boulogne, were blown. Told me of some half-pay English officers, who having exhausted all other means of raising the wind, at last levied subscriptions for a private theatre, and having announced the *Forty Thieves* for the first representation, absconded on the morning of the day with the money. Our passage only four hours, but very disagreeable.

May 14 [IN PARIS] Rogers told me a good deal about Lord Byron, whom he saw both going and coming back. Expressed to R. the same contempt for Shakspeare which he has often expressed to me; treats his companion Shelley very cavalierly. By the bye, I find (by a letter received within these few days, by Horace Smith), that Lord B. showed Shelley the letters I wrote on the subject of his *Cain*, warning him against the influence Shelley's admiration might have over his mind, and deprecating that wretched display of atheism which Shelley had given in to, and in which Lord B. himself seemed but too much inclined to follow him. Shelley, too, has written anxiously to Smith to say how sorry he should be to stand ill in my opinion, and making some explanation of his opinions which Smith is to show me. Rogers starts for England to-morrow morning.

July 17 [IN PARIS] Received to-day a letter from Brougham, inclosing one from Barnes (the editor of *The Times*), proposing that, as he is ill, I shall take his place for some time in writing the leading articles of that paper; the pay to be £100. a month. This is flattering. To be thought capable of wielding so powerful a political machine as *The Times* newspaper is a tribute the more flattering (as is usually the case) from my feeling conscious that I do not deserve it....

July 18 Wrote to decline the proposal of *The Times*.

August 5 [IN PARIS] Called on Bryan; thence to Lafitte's, where, in talking of the disgraceful outrage on the English actors last week, somebody said, that in Buonaparte's time, when there was a violent opposition to a play called *Christophe Colomb* (merely because it was written in violation of rules of the critics), Napoleon sent down to the theatre, not only some troops of gens-d'armerie, but a piece of artillery, and carried the tragedy off smoothly. What a powerful support at an author's back.

November 11 [IN PARIS] The dinner took place at Robert's; about fifty sat down: Lord Trimlestown in the chair: among the company were Lord Granard, Sir G. Webster, Robert Adair, &c. Collinet's band attended; the dinner one of Robert's best; and all went off remarkably well. In returning thanks for my health, I gave "Prosperity to England," with an eulogium on the moral worth of that country, which was felt more, both by myself and the company, from its being delivered in France, and produced much effect. Douglas, in proposing Bessy's health, after praising her numerous virtues, &c. &c., concluded thus:—"We need not, therefore, gentlemen, be surprised that Mr Moore is about to communicate to the world 'The Loves of the Angels,' having been so long familiar with one at home." In returning thanks for this, I mentioned the circumstance of the village bells welcoming her arrival, as being *her* triumph in England, while I had mine this day in France, and concluded thus:—"These, gentlemen, are rewards and atonements for everything. No matter how poor I may steal through life—no matter how many calamities (even heavier than that from which I have now been relieved) may fall upon me—as long as such friends as you hold out the hand of fellowship to me at parting, and the sound of honest English bells shall welcome me and mine at meeting, I shall consider myself a Crœsus in that best wealth, happiness, and shall lay down my head, grateful for the gifts God has given." In introducing the subject of the village bells, I said, "This is a day of vanity for me; and you, who set the fountain running, ought not to complain of its overflowing." Lattin proposed the health of my father and mother, and mentioned the delight he had felt in witnessing my father's triumph at the dinner in Dublin. In returning thanks for this, I alluded to Southey's making his Kehama enter triumphantly in through seven gates at the same moment, and said: "This miraculous multiplication of one gentleman into seven has been, to a great degree, effected by the toasts into which your kindness has subdivided me this day": concluding thus;—"I have often, gentlemen, heard of sympathetic ink, but here is a liquid which has much better claims to that epithet; and if there is a glass of such at this moment before my good old father, it must,

I think, sparkle in sympathetic reply to those which you have done him the honour of filling to him." A song was sung by Grattan during the night, which he had written for the occasion. Left them between one and two, and went to Douglas's, where I supped.

December 19 [IN LONDON] Took my place for Sunday in the York House coach. Made an agreement for a hackney coach, and went out to Hornsey to visit the grave of our poor child Barbara, Bessy having heard it was much neglected. Found this not to be the case. Sought out the sexton, and bid him have it new sodded, giving him at the same time five shillings, and promising him more when I should come again.

December 26 Rather fidgetty about the fate of my book. Bessy had a note yesterday from Lady L. with a present of some toys for the children, but not a word about the *Angels*. Rather ominous this. Wrote to Lady Donegal yesterday about some silver tissue for Mrs Phipps's dress for the fancy ball, and said, "Don't say a word about the *Angels* in your answer; stick to the silver tissue."

December 27 An answer from Lady Donegal with the following sentence in it, which, from the state of nervousness I had got into about my book, came upon me like a thunderbolt. "You bid me not say anything about the *Angels*, but I must so far disobey you as to say that I am both vexed and disappointed, and I think that you will feel I am right in not allowing Barbara to read it." I never remember anything that gave me much more pain than this. It seemed at once to ring the death-knell of my poem. This at once accounted for the dead silence of the Longmans since the publication, for the non-appearance of the second edition, which I was taught to expect would be announced the third day, for Lord Lansdowne's reserve on the subject, for everything. My book, then, was considered (why or wherefore it was in vain to inquire) improper, and what I thought the best, as well as the most moral thing I had ever written, was to be doomed to rank with the rubbish of Carlile[1] and Co. for ever. Bowles, who was with me at the time, endeavoured most good-humouredly to soothe me, and, though he had not read the poem, gallantly made himself responsible that I could not have written anything to bring upon me such a censure. It was all in vain. I wrote off to the Longmans to beg they would tell me the worst at once, and to my mother, to prepare her for the failure which I now considered as certain. In this mood Bowles left me, and in about an hour after, luckily for my peace of mind, Lord Lansdowne and Byng arrived. Their coming was like an avatar to me. Lord L. declared, in the warmest manner, that he thought the poem not only beautiful, but perfectly unexceptional and pure, and that he had no hesitation in preferring it to anything I had ever written. Byng too (who two or three weeks since had expressed himself with some degree of alarm about the title), told me that, on reading the poem, he had

[1] Richard Carlile, the publisher of works of an infidel character. [Lord John Russell's Note.]

instantly written off to some friends who felt the same apprehensions as himself, that "it might be safely trusted in the nursery." It is inconceivable the relief all this was to me, and not less so to my darling Bessy, who had seen the wretched state I was thrown into by Lady D.'s letter, and had in vain employed her good sense and sweetness to counteract its effect. Walked part of the way back with Lord L. and B.

January 14 Dinner very agreeable. Miss N. mentioned a French lady, of whom she inquired, by way of compliment, "in what manner she had contrived to speak English so well?" and the answer was, "I begun by *traducing*." Lord L. in the evening, quoted a ridiculous passage from the preface to Mrs Piozzi's *Retrospections*, in which, anticipating the ultimate perfection of the human race, she says she does not despair of the time arriving "when Vice will take refuge in the arms of Impossibility." Mentioned also an Ode of hers to Posterity, beginning, "Posterity, gregarious Dame"; the only meaning of which must be, a Lady *chez qui* numbers assemble,—a Lady *at home*. I repeated what Jekyll told me the other day of Bearcroft, saying to Mrs Piozzi, when Thrale, after she had called him frequently Mr Beercraft, "Beercraft is not my name, Madam; it may be *your* trade, but it is not *my name*."

April 1 [IN LONDON] Saw Sir A. Cooper, who apologised for "giving *such a man* the trouble" of coming to him. Said there was no cause for uneasiness in the symptoms I felt. Recommended me, among other things, the use of the shower-bath. Begged me to let him see me again, "as a friend, if I would do him that honour." Altogether very courteous. Walked afterwards (for the first time since I came to town) to Rogers's. Very agreeable. Asked me to dine with him, which I did; company, Wordsworth and his wife and sister-in-law, Cary (the translator of Dante), Hallam, and Sharpe. Some discussion about Racine and Voltaire, in which I startled, and rather shocked them, by saying that, though there could be no doubt of the superior taste and workmanship of Racine, yet that Voltaire's tragedies *interested* me the most of the two. Another electrifying assertion of mine was, that I would much rather see *Othello* and *Romeo and Juliet* as Italian operas, and played by *Pasta*, than the original of Shakspeare, as acted on the London stage. Wordsworth told of some acquaintance of his, who being told, among other things, to go and see the *Chapeau de Paille* at Antwerp, said, on his return, "I saw all the other things you mentioned, but as for the straw-hat manufactory I could not make it out."

April 3 Dined at Longmans; Power of the party. They mentioned, as a proof of Walter Scott's industry, that when he was editor of the *Edinburgh Annual Register*, being allowed books, as is the custom, to cut up for extracts, &c., he would often, in order to save a book worth 15*s*. for his library, pass the greater part of the day transcribing the necessary passages.

April 4 Dined at Mr Monkhouse's (a gentleman I had never seen before), on Wordsworth's invitation, who lives there whenever he comes to town. A singular party: Coleridge, Rogers, Wordsworth and wife, Charles Lamb (the hero, at present, of the *London Magazine*) and his sister (the poor woman who went mad with him in the diligence on the way to Paris), and a Mr Robinson[1], one of the *minora sidera* of this constellation of the Lakes, the host himself, a Mæcenas of the school, contributing nothing but good dinners and silence. Charles Lamb a clever fellow certainly; but full of villainous and abortive puns, which he miscarries of every minute. Some excellent things, however, have come from him; and his friend Robinson mentioned to me not a bad one. On Robinson's receiving his first brief, he called upon Lamb to tell him of it. "I suppose," said Lamb, "you addressed that line of Pope's to it, 'Thou great *first cause*, least understood.'" Coleridge told some tolerable things. One of a poor author, who, on receiving from his publisher an account of the proceeds (as he expected it to be) of a work he had published, saw among the items, "Cellarage, £3. 10s. 6d." and thought it was a charge for the trouble of *selling* the 700 copies, which he did not consider unreasonable; but on inquiry he found it was for the *cellar*-room occupied by his work, not a copy of which had stirred from thence. He told, too, of the servant-maid where he himself had lodged at Ramsgate, coming in to say that he was wanted, there being a person at the door inquiring for a poet; and on his going out, he found it was a pot-boy from the public house, whose cry, of "any *pots* for the Angel," the girl had mistaken for a demand for a *poet*. Im-

[1] Henry Crabb Robinson (1775–1867), the famous diarist.

probable enough. In talking of Klopstock, he mentioned his description of the Deity's "head spreading through space," which, he said, gave one the idea of a hydrocephalous affection. Lamb quoted an epitaph by Clio Rickman, in which, after several lines, in the usual jog-trot style of epitaph, he continued thus:

> He well performed the husband's, father's part,
> And knew immortal Hudibras by heart.

A good deal of talk with Lamb about De Foe's works, which he praised warmly, particularly *Colonel Jack*, of which he mentioned some striking passages. Is collecting the works of the Dunciad heroes. Coleridge said that Spencer is the poet most remarkable for contrivances of versification: his spelling words differently, to suit the music of the line, putting sometimes "spake," sometimes "spoke," as it fell best on the ear, &c. &c. To show the difference in the facility of reciting verses, according as they were skilfully or unskilfully constructed, he said he had made the experiment upon *Beppo* and *Whistlecraft* (Frere's poem), and found that he could read three stanzas of the latter in the same time as two of the former. This is absurd. Talked much of Jeremy Taylor; his work upon "Prophesying," &c. C. Lamb told me he had got £170. for his two years contributions to the *London Magazine* (Letters of Elia). Should have thought it more.

April 9 Dined at Power's, to meet Bishop. Jackson, the boxer, had called upon me in the morning, to know where that well-known line, "Men are but children of a larger growth," is to be found; said there was a bet depending on it, and he thought I would be most likely to tell. Not, he said, in Young's *Night Thoughts*. Promised to make out, if I could.

April 10 Dined at Rogers's. A distinguished party: S. Smith, Ward, Luttrell, Payne Knight, Lord Aberdeen, Abercromby, Lord Clifden, &c. Smith[1] particularly amusing. Have rather held out against him hitherto: but this day he conquered me; and I now am his victim, in the laughing way, for life. His imagination of a duel between two doctors, with oil of croton on the tips of their fingers, trying to touch each other's lips, highly ludicrous. What Rogers says of Smith, very true, that whenever the conversation is getting dull, he throws in some touch which makes it rebound, and rise again as light as ever. Ward's[2] artificial efforts, which to me are always painful, made still more so by their contrast to Smith's natural and overflowing exuberance. Luttrell, too, considerably extinguished to-day; but there is this difference between Luttrell and Smith—that after the former, you remember what good things he said, and after the latter, you merely remember how much you laughed.

April 14 Received an impatient letter from Bess, which rather disturbed me, both on her account and my own. Perceive she is getting quite uncomfortable without me,

---

[1] Rev. Sydney Smith (1771–1845), miscellaneous writer, renowned as a wit.
[2] Robert Plumer Ward (1765–1846), politician and novelist, author of *Tremaine*.

and yet have quantities of things to do in town. Must manage as well as I can.

May 24 My darling girl's symptoms became decisive after breakfast; a message was despatched for the midwife; and, in little more than half an hour after she arrived, a little boy was born. Added a few lines announcing the event to several letters of Bessy's, which she had left open for the purpose, and wrote two or three myself.

May 25 Bessy doing marvellously well, and the little fright (as all such young things are) prospering also. Wrote several letters.

May 28 Being my birthday, dined in my dear Bessy's bed-room, who still keeps wonderfully well.

May 30 Set off in Phipps's gig for Melksham; found there that I had left all my money at home; borrowed a pound of P.'s coachman, and sent a note by him to Bessy, to forward me the money by the evening coach to Bath. Arrived, by the Devizes coach, at Bath at eleven o'clock. Called immediately on my darling Anastasia, at Miss Furness's; took her out to walk. Showed me a pretty way through the fields. Sweet child! I could not help stopping every instant to look at her and kiss her. Weather very hot. Left her at home, and walked about Bath; saw my name placarded on the walls everywhere.

June 3 Breakfasted with Rogers; Constable, of Edinburgh, the great publisher, and Bowles, of the party. In talking of the craft of bookselling, Constable said, "Mr Moore, if you will let me have a poem from your pen, I will engage to sell thrice as many copies as the Longmans ever did, even of *Lalla Rookh*." Very encouraging this, and comes seasonably to put me in better conceit with myself. In conversing with me afterwards, he intimated his strong wish that I should connect myself with the *Edinburgh Review*. In talking of Walter Scott, and the author of *Waverley*, he continually forgot himself, and made them the same person. Has had the original MS. of the novels presented to him by the author, in forty-nine volumes, written with his own hand; very few corrections. Says the author to his knowledge has already received more than a hundred thousand pounds for his novels alone. Walter Scott apparently very idle; the only time he is known to begin to study is about three hours in the morning before breakfast; the rest of the day he is at the disposal of everybody, and rarely retires at night till others do. Went with Constable and Bowles to Sir George Beaumont's.

June 19 Breakfasted with Rogers: only Kenny; Creevey did not come. Went with Kenny to hear him read his new piece to the actors at the Haymarket; rehearsal of *Figaro* going on: very amusing altogether. ... Dreamt last night that I saw Bessy falling out of a gig; and find, from her letter, that she and Mrs Phipps were to drive in our new pony carriage to-day to Buckhill: wrote to her (as indeed I had done before) to beg she would not drive out any more till my return.

June 21 Called, by appointment, on Constable; long conversation with him; most anxious that I should come to Edinburgh; and promises that I shall prosper there. The *Review* (he told me in confidence) is sinking; Jeffrey[1] has not time enough to devote to it; would be most happy to have me in his place; but the resignation must come from himself, as the proprietors could not propose it to him. Jeffrey has £700. a year for being editor, and the power of drawing £2800. for contributors. Told him that I could not think of undertaking the editorship under a £1000. a year, as I should, if I undertook it, devote myself almost entirely to it, and less than a £1000. would not pay me for this. He seemed to think that if Jeffrey was once out of the way, there would be no difficulty about terms; read me a letter he had just received from his partner on the subject, in which he says, "Moore is out of all sight the best man we could have; his name would revive the reputation of the *Review*; he would continue to us our connection with the old contributors, and the work would become more literary and more regular; but we must get him gradually into it; and the first step is to persuade him to come to Edinburgh." All this (evidently not intended to be seen by me) is very flattering.

June 24 Off in the coach at six; a very pretty person of the party. Arrived at Calne a little after five, and

[1] Francis Jeffrey (1773–1850) edited the *Edinburgh Review* from its commencement in 1802 until 1829. In 1806, in consequence of a severe attack upon Moore's verse by Jeffrey, the two arranged to fight a duel at Chalk Farm, but the police intervened and the two men of letters soon became friends.

expected to find our new carriage (as Bessy promised) in waiting for me. Set off to walk home; met our man William on the way, who told me that the carriage could not come on account of something that was the matter with the harness. Sent him on to Calne, and walked home, which I found rather fatiguing after my sleepless night. Met by Bessy at the door, looking very ill, and her face and nose much disfigured; upon inquiry the secret came out, that on Sunday evening (the evening before last), she and Mrs Phipps and Tom drove out in the little carriage (which Bessy herself had driven two or three times before), and in going down by Sandridge Lodge the pony, from being bitten, they think, by a forest-fly, set off galloping and kicking, without any possibility of being reined in, threw them all into a ditch, ran off with the carriage to Bromham, and knocked both it and himself almost to pieces. Much shocked and mortified, though grateful to God that it had not been worse. Bessy, in protecting little Tom in her arms, came with her unlucky nose to the ground, which is much swollen, though (as Dr Headly says, who has seen it) not broken. The rest of the party escaped with some bruises. What a strange coincidence with my dream! It was a great effort for me to compass the expense of this little luxury; and such is the end of it.

November 15 Dined at Phipps's; though Bessy at first refused, this being her birthday, and it having long been a fancy of hers that she was to die at the age of thirty, which she completed to-day. Company, the Bowleses, Lockes, Dr Starkey, Mr Fisher, Edmonston, &c.

November 16 My dear girl, who acknowledged that the fancy about her dying at thirty had haunted her a good deal, gave me a letter which she had written to me in contemplation of this event; full of such things as, in spite of my efforts to laugh at her for her nonsense, made me cry.

December 14 Received a note from Croker, proposing that I should belong to a new club[1] for literary and scientific persons, to be formed on the model of the United Service, &c. Wishes me to propose it to Lord Lansdowne also, and says, "We should not feel that we did our duty to the proposed institution if we did not express to Lord Lansdowne and to you the wish of all the present members of the Committee that his Lordship and you should belong to us."

April 3 Breakfasted with Newton, in order to meet Russell the actor, who had promised me a dress to take down with me to Bath, Bessy having expressed a wish to go to a masquerade there on Monday, and I having agreed to meet her in Bath for the purpose. Excellent this; having an appointment with my wife at a masquerade! Promised me a Figaro's dress.

April 5 Bessy and Tom arrived between eleven and twelve. The dear girl has not been at all well for some weeks, but as brisk and alive as usual, notwithstanding. Went to see dear Anastasia, and took her and Julia Starkey to see the panorama of the Coronation; ordered

[1] The "Athenæum."

our dominoes for the night, *my* Figaro dress being given up. Dined at Mr T. Phipps's; home and dressed. The masquerade, as a spectacle, beautiful, and when we were allowed to cast off our masks very agreeable; the room, with the booths for refreshments on each side, better imagined and managed than anything of the kind I ever saw, and no expense spared to make all perfect. Bessy delighted; and danced towards the end of the night with Tom Bayly. Not home till between six and seven in the morning.

May 11 Breakfasted at Newton's with Lockhart; found him agreeable. Told of Sir W. Scott once finding Crabbe and some Scotch chieftain (in his full costume) trying to converse together in French, Crabbe having taken the tartan hero for a foreigner, and the other, on being addressed in French by Crabbe, supposing him to be an Italian abbé.

May 12 ...Went to the Literary Fund Dinner, of which I was a steward. Surprised on finding so large a portion of its directors and visitors to be persons whose names I had never heard before; in short, the only downright *literati* among them were myself and old George Dyer, the poet, who used to take advantage of the people being earthed up to the chin by Dr Graham, to go and read his verses to them. Lord Lansdowne in the chair, and Lord John Russell next him; I sat opposite to them. Lord L. gave my health in a most flattering manner, and nothing could be more warm than the reception it met with from the company;

made them a long speech, which was interrupted at almost every sentence by applauses.

May 14 ... Calling at Colburn's library to inquire the address of the editor of the *Literary Gazette*, was told by the shopman that Lord Byron was dead. Could not believe it, but feared the worst, as his last letter to me about a fortnight since mentioned the severe attack of apoplexy or epilepsy which he had just suffered. Hurried to inquire. Met Lord Lansdowne, who said he feared it was but too true. Recollected then the unfinished state in which my agreement for the redemption of the "Memoirs" lay. Lord L. said, "You have nothing but Murray's fairness to depend upon." Went off to the *Morning Chronicle* office, and saw the *Courier*, which confirmed this most disastrous news. Hastened to Murray's, who was denied to me, but left a note for him, to say that "in consequence of this melancholy event, I had called to know when it would be convenient to him to complete the arrangements with respect to the 'Memoirs,' which we had agreed upon between us when I was last in town." Sent an apology to Lord King, with whom I was to have dined. A note from Hobhouse (which had been lying some time for me) announcing the event. Called upon Rogers, who had not heard the news. Remember his having, in the same manner, found me unacquainted with Lord Nelson's death, late on the day when the intelligence arrived. Advised me not to stir at all on the subject of the "Memoirs," but to wait and see what Murray would do; and in the meantime to ask Brougham's opinion. Dined alone at the George, and in the evening left a note for Brougham. Found a note on my return home from Douglas Kinnaird, anxiously inquiring in whose possession the "Memoirs" were, and saying that he was ready, on the part of Lord Byron's family, to advance the two thousand pounds for the MS., in order to give Lady Byron and the rest of the family an opportunity of deciding whether they wished them to be published or no.

July 12 Was with Rogers at half-past eight. Set off for George Street, Westminster, at half-past nine. When I approached the house, and saw the crowd assembled, felt a nervous trembling come over me, which lasted till the whole ceremony was over; thought I should be ill. Never was at a funeral before, but poor Curran's. The riotous curiosity of the mob, the bustle of the undertakers, &c., and all the other vulgar accompaniments of the ceremony, mixing with my recollections of him who was gone, produced a combination of disgust and sadness that was deeply painful to me. Hobhouse, in the active part he had to sustain, showed a manly, unaffected feeling. Our coachful consisted of Rogers, Campbell, Colonel Stanhope, Orlando (the Greek deputy), and myself. Saw a lady crying in a barouche as we turned out of George Street, and said to myself, "Bless her heart, whoever she is!" There were, however, few respectable persons among the crowd; and the whole ceremony was anything but what it ought to have been. Left the hearse as soon as it was off the stones, and returned home to get rid of my black clothes, and try to forget, as much as possible, the wretched feelings I had experienced in them. Stanhope said in the coach, in speaking of the strange mixture of avarice and profusion which Byron exhibited, that he had heard himself say, "He was sure he should die a miser and a bigot." Hobhouse, to-day, mentioned as remarkable, the change in Byron's character when he went to Greece. Finding that there was ardour enough among them, but that steadiness was what they wanted, he instantly took a quiet and passive tone, listening to the different representations made to him, and letting his judgment be properly informed, before he either urged or took any decided course of action. Fixed with Stanhope to come to breakfast with Rogers on Wednesday. Walked with R. into the park, and met a soldier's funeral, which, in the full state my heart was in, affected me strongly. The air the bugles played was, "I'm wearing awa, like snow-wreaths in the thaw." Went to Mrs Story's, and supped with her. I and the girls went to Vauxhall: a most delicious night. Rogers told me of Burke taking a tour on foot with his brother, and when they came to two branching roads Burke held up his stick to decide which they should take. The stick said Bath. Burke went there and was married.

July 14 Breakfasted with Rogers to meet Leicester Stanhope. Much talk about Lord Byron, of whom Stanhope saw a good deal at Missolonghi. Byron entirely guided in his views by Mavrocordato; "a mere puppet in his hands;" Mavrocordato always teazing him for money, till Byron hated the very sight of him.

The story of Byron's giving four thousand pounds to raise the siege of Missolonghi not true. A little money goes an immense way in Greece. A hundred pounds might sometimes be the means of keeping a fleet or army together. Mavrocordato appointed B. to command the army of western Greece. Stanhope thought this appointment of a stranger injurious to the dignity of the Greek nation, and told B. so, which annoyed him. S. expressed the same to some members of the Greek government, who said it was done by Mavrocordato, without consulting them. In the passage from Cephalonia, the ship, aboard which were Count Gambia, Byron's servants, packages, &c. &c., was taken and carried into a Turkish port; but, by some management, got off again. Byron himself, next morning, at break of day, got close in with a Turkish frigate, which, however, took his small vessel for a fire-ship and sheered off. B. gave but little money. After his severe attack, when he was lying nervous and reduced in bed, insurrection took place among the Suliots, who would frequently rush into his bedroom to make their remonstrances. Byron would not have them shut out, but always listened to them with much good nature; very gallant this. Asked Stanhope as to his courage, which I have sometimes heard the depreciating gossips of society throw a doubt upon; and not long ago, indeed, was told of Lord Bathurst's saying, when somebody expressed an apprehension for Lord Byron's safety in Greece, "Oh, never fear, he will not expose himself to much danger." Stanhope said, on the contrary, he was always for rushing into danger; would propose one day to go in a fire-ship; another time, to storm Lepanto; would however, laugh at all this himself afterwards, and say he wished that—(some one, I don't know whom, that was expected to take a command) would come and supersede him. Stanhope had several stormy conversations with him on business. In one of them Byron threatened to write a pasquinade against him; and Stanhope begged him to do so, and he would give him a hundred pounds for the copyright. Still it was an extraordinary scene when the leeches had bit the temporal artery in his first attack; the two physicians squabbling over him, and he, weak as he was, joking at their expense. Capt. Parry was his favourite *butt* at Missolonghi.

July 17 With Kenny a little after ten. Mrs Shelley[1] very gentle and feminine. Spoke a good deal of Byron; his treatment of Leigh Hunt, by her account, not very good. Made some remarks upon him in a letter to Murray, which reached Hunt's ears, and produced an expostulation from him to Byron on the subject; B.'s answer aristocratical and evasive. The Guiccioli refused a settlement from him (ten thousand pounds, I think). Spoke of the story of the girl in the *Giaour*. Founded (as B. has often told me) on the circumstance of a young girl, whom he knew himself in Greece, and whom he supposed to be a Greek, but who proved to be a Turk; and who underwent on his account the punishment mentioned in the poem; he met her body carried along in the sack. Kenny to-day mentioned

[1] Mary Shelley, wife of the poet.

Charles Lamb's being once bored by a lady praising to him "such a charming man!" &c. &c. ending with "I know him, bless him!" on which Lamb, said "Well, I don't but d——n him, at a hazard."

July 19 ... Hobhouse, at Byron's funeral, told me that he looked at the corpse at Hanson's desire, who thought it necessary some one besides himself should see it, and that there was hardly a trace of identity left. Could hardly believe it was he; the mustachios, the puffy face, the shaggy eye-brows, &c. The brains weighed a third or fourth more than is usual.

August 3 ... In the evening talked with Lord Holland about Sheridan. Burke, though very magnanimous in forwarding Mr Fox when he appeared in the arena of politics, did not feel the same towards Sheridan, but regarded him with great jealousy. Sheridan's strong wish to make his power felt in politics grew still stronger in his latter days from vanity and disappointment. Lord H. knows of no regular application from S. to see Mr Fox when he was dying; never heard of his refusing to see him; though, at the same time, is sure that he would not have liked it. Thinks Sheridan was slow in argument; did not all at once see your drift.

October 23 Dined at Bowood: company, Grosetts and Clutterbucks; Mrs Clutterbuck looking very pretty. Clutterbuck's story of the old lady (his aunt) excellent. Being very nervous, she told Sir W. Farquhar she thought Bath would do her good. "It's very odd," says Sir W., "but that's the very thing I was going to recommend to you. I will write the particulars of your case to a very clever man there, in whose hands you will be well taken care of." The lady, furnished with the letter, sets off, and on arriving at Newbury, feeling as usual, very nervous, she said to her confidant, "Long as Sir Walter has attended me, he has never explained to me what ails me. I have a great mind to open his letter and see what he has stated of my case to the Bath physician." In vain her friend represented to her the breach of confidence this would be. She opened the letter, and read, "Dear Davis, keep the old lady three weeks, and send her back again."

October 24 A good deal of talk at breakfast about the falsehoods and misrepresentations in Medwin's book about Byron. Told them the whole particulars of my first acquaintance with Byron, and the mis-statement about the "leadless bullet" that led to it. Lord L. owned he himself had been always under the impression that the story was true, and that the pistols in my meeting with Jeffrey were really *not* loaded. A proof what a fast hold the world takes of anything that disparages. He mentioned that the present Lords Hertford and Mansfield, when at the University, were mischievously set to fight in a room, by their seconds, and made to fire twice; the seconds not having loaded either pistol, and even having contrived a hole in the wainscot to make them think, after the first fire, that it was where the bullet went through. Walked to Buckhill to see Bessy, who slept there last night. Went with her some part of her way home, and then returned to Bowood. Dressed, and set off with Lord L. to dinner at Bowles's. Company, Bingham, Linley, Lord L., Phipps, and myself. Bowles mentioned that at some celebration at Reading school, when the patrons or governors of it (beer and brandy merchants) were to be welcomed with a Latin address, the boy appointed to the task thus bespoke them, "*Salvete, hospites Cele*beer*imi*," and then turning to the others, "*Salvete, hospites cele*brandi."

December 15 ... Called upon Hobhouse. Much talk with him about the various Byroniana since we last met. It was Sir F. Burdett who advised him to withdraw his pamphlet in answer to Medwin, which he had printed and announced. Showed me some proofs of old Dallas's manœuvring from Lord Byron's letters. Told him (what I feel), that all that has happened since the destruction of the "Memoirs" convinces me that he was right in advising their total suppression, as, if the remainder were published, much more mischief would be imagined to have existed in the suppressed part than there is even now. Begged of him to give me some time or other under his hand, for my own satisfaction, the assurance which had such weight with me in giving up the "Memoirs," that Byron had expressed to him, when they last met, his regret at having put them out of his own power, and that it was only delicacy towards me that prevented him from recalling them; said that I might depend upon it that he would. Went to the Hollands; Brougham, Mackintosh, and

Lord Sefton. Some talk with Mackintosh; said he believed Tooke had assisted Paine in his answer to Burke. Mentioned, as like Tooke's manner, the passage about a king having a million a year; his only duty being to receive the salary. I must see this passage, in which he objected to the word "nominal," as incumbering the point.

December 23 Off in the coach at quarter-past six. Had for one of my companions a clergyman, brother of the Sherer who wrote *Recollections in the Peninsular*, &c. &c. An odd and an amusing person; quoted a neat remark of Lardner's on predestination, "If we were judged before we were born, then certainly we were never born to be judged." Found all pretty well at home, and my dearest Anastasia among the rest for her holidays. Sherer said the Longmans had told his brother that I had the most generous contempt for money of any man they ever met.

December 25 Eat my plum pudding at home. Dined at two on account of the servants, who were indulged with a dinner for their friends (about a dozen of them) and a large party in the evening. Very jolly and uproarious till twelve o'clock.

December 29 Company at Bowood, Lord Auckland and the Misses Eden, Sir John Newport, Macdonald, Mr Baring Wall, and Hallam. Mentioned Gilbert Wakefield's taking Pope's "Gently spread thy purple pinions" as serious, and saying that it was not in Mr Pope's happiest style. Sung in the evening. In talking of my own compositions, mentioned the tendency I had sometimes to run into consecutive fifths, and adding, sometime after, that Bishop was the person who now revised my music, Lord Auckland said, "Other Bishops take care of the tithes, but he looks after the fifths." A good story of a man brimful of ill-temper, coming out of a room where he had lost all his money at play, and seeing a person (a perfect stranger to him) tying his shoe at the top of the stairs: " D—n you (says he), you're always tying your shoe," and kicked him down stairs. Slept there.

January 12 Recollect some other things Mackintosh said. Wilberforce's good remark about the Catholics, that they were "like persons discharged from prison, but still wearing the prison dress." Mentioned an advertisement that appeared in 1792: "Wanted for a King of France, an easy good-tempered man, who can bear confinement, and has no followers." Wilberforce was made a citizen by the French Convention, and Courteney, who was in Paris at the time, said, " If you make Mr W. a citizen, they will take you for an assemblage of negroes, for it is well known he never favoured the liberty of any white man in all his life." Dr Thomson said of Godwin (who in the full pride of his theory of perfectibility, said he "could educate tigers,") "I should like to see him in a cage with two of his pupils."

January 21 Lord Lansdowne at breakfast mentioned of Dutens, who wrote the *Memoires d'un Voyageur qui se repose*, and was a great antiquarian, that on his describing once his good luck in having found (what he fancied to be) a tooth of Scipio's, in Italy, some one asked him what he had done with it, upon which he answered briskly, "What have I done with it? *la voici*," pointing to his mouth, where he had made it supplemental to a lost one of his own. The Lansdownes off to Bath after breakfast, and I (after singing a little for the girls) followed them with Col. Houlton. The grand opening to-day of the Literary Institution of Bath. Attended the inaugural lecture by Sir G. Gibbs at two. Walked about a little afterwards, and to the dinner at six: Lord Lansdowne in the chair. Two Bishops present; and about 180 persons altogether. Bowles and Crabbe of the number. Lord L. alluded to us in his first speech, as among the literary ornaments, if not of Bath itself, of its precincts; and in describing our respective characteristics, said, beginning with me, "the one, a specimen of the most glowing, animated, and impassioned style," &c.; this word "impassioned" spoken out very strongly in the very ear of the Bishop of Bath and Wells, who sat next him. On the healths of the three poets being given, though much called for, I did not rise, but motioned to Crabbe, who got up and said a few words. When it came to my turn to rise, such a burst of enthusiasm received me as I could not but feel proud of. Spoke for some time, and with much success. Concluded by some tributes to Crabbe and Bowles, and said of the latter, that "his poetry was the first fountain at which I had drunk the pure freshness of the English language, and learned (however little I might have profited by my learning) of what variety of sweetness the music of English verse is capable."

May 28 My birthday. What, again! well, the more the merrier; at least I hope so; and, as yet (with all my difficulties), have no reason to complain. An excellent, warm-hearted, lively wife, and dear, promising children. What more need I ask for? A little addition of health to the wife, and wealth to the husband, would make all perfect. Prepared for my trip to town to-morrow.

June 2 Dressed early (having to dine at Holland House), for the purpose of meeting Bessy at the coach. Mrs Story took me, and after our waiting some time at Knightsbridge, the Bath coach arrived with Bessy, Tom and Mary Dalby. Deposited the two former at Mrs Story's, and proceeded to Holland House. Sat next my Lady, who was very gracious, filled my glass amply with champagne, and descanted on the merits and prices of Rudesheim, Johannisberg, and Hochheim. Said to me during dinner, "This will be a dull book of yours, this 'Sheridan,' I fear." "On the contrary," I replied, "it will be a very lively, amusing book! not from my part in it, but," &c. &c. In the evening Lady Lansdowne came, looking so handsome and so good, that it was quite comfortable to see her. Told her of Bessy's arrival. "Then she'll come to me," she said, "on Saturday evening." "Bessy," I answered, "has brought no evening things, for the express purpose of *not* going anywhere." After a short pause she turned round, in her lively way, and said, "I'll tell you what: bring Mrs Moore to see me to-morrow morning, and she shall have the choice of my wardrobe: I assure you it's a very convenient one, fits both fat and lean. I once dressed out four girls for a ball, and there were four gowns of mine dancing about the room all night."

June 8 Up at five; and saw my treasures safe in the coach. Returned, and went to sleep again for an hour and a half. Had Mr Smyth (the professor) with me while I breakfasted. Told me a great deal about his connection with Sheridan....Smyth, one day, while looking over his table, while waiting to catch him coming out of his bedroom, saw several unopened letters, one with a coronet, and said to Wesley, "We are all treated alike." Upon which Wesley told him that he had once found amongst the unopened heap a letter of his own to Sheridan, which he knew contained a ten pound note, sent by him to release S. from some inn where he was "money bound," and that he opened it, and took out the money. Wesley, said, also, that the butler assured him he found once the window-frames stuffed with papers to prevent them from rattling, and, on taking them out, saw they were bank notes, which S. had used for this purpose some stormy night and never missed them.

July 26 The whole of this next month was devoted, with little interruption, to my "Sheridan" task, correcting proofs, and finishing what yet remained to be written. Found at home, on my arrival, an extract from Dr Parr's will, sent me by his executors, in which he says, "I give a ring to Thomas Moore, of Sloperton, Wilts, who stands high in my estimation for original genius, for his exquisite sensibility, for his independent spirit, and incorruptible integrity." During the hot weather of this month, July (hotter than any remembered for many years), we were imprudent enough to have parties for the children on several of the most sultry evenings, at our own house, Prowse's (the curate, who has four or five little ones), and Phipps's: blindman's buff, and racing in such weather, was but ill likely to do either old or young any good; none, however, suffered by it except Bessy, her leg not getting at all well. Towards the end of July the Lansdownes arrived. Bessy left home for Cheltenham on the 22nd, where Lady Donegal had provided lodgings for her, and Bowles took her and the two little ones (Tom and Russell) in his carriage.

August 26 Drove with Lord Essex and Lady Davy to call on Lady Elizabeth Whitbread, who was on a visit in the neighbourhood. On our return sung to Lady Davy. She talked much of the Guiccioli, whom she knew intimately at Rome. Saw a note in a book of hers which she had lent Lord Byron, in which he said that it was his strong wish to believe that she would continue to love him, but there were three things against it, "she was nineteen, come out of a convent, and a woman." Lord E. asked me to take a drive with him through the grounds, which I most readily accepted; full of beauty. Showed me one or two cottages, and said he had many others to tempt me with, if I would come and live in his neighbourhood. Told me of his having taken Sheridan to Drury Lane, the first and only time he ever set foot in the new theatre, and (according to Lord E.'s account) the last time he ever was out of his house before his death. The actors drank his health in the green-room most flatteringly. Told the anecdote of the Prince pitching the Abbé St Phar (half-brother to the Duke of Orleans) into the water at Newmarket. The Abbé had some method of making the fish lie still by tickling (or some such manœuvre), and proceeded to exhibit his skill, having first made the Prince and all the rest give their honours that they would not push him into the water. He then bent down to the river or pond, when the P., not being able to resist the temptation, pitched him head over heels into the middle of it. The Abbé was so enraged, that when he got out, he ran after the Prince, and but that the company favoured the escape of the latter, would have treated him rather roughly. The Prince once having applied, in speaking of Sumner (now member for Surrey), a cant phrase he was much in the habit of using, some one told Sumner, who, meeting Jack Payne afterwards in the street, said to him, showing a large stick he had in his hand, "Tell your master he had better keep out of my way, as, if I meet him, I shall fell him to the earth." When Fox questioned the Prince about the loan from the Duke of Orleans, and the bonds which the Prince had given for the purpose, the Prince denied most solemnly having ever given any bonds; upon which Fox produced them to him out of his pocket, thus convicting him of a lie to his very face. Errington was the person supposed to have been present at the marriage of the Prince and Mrs Fitzherbert. When Lord Essex returned once from France, the Prince said to him, "I am told, but cannot believe it, that when at Paris you wear strings to your shoes." "It is very true, sir, and so does the Duke of Orleans, &c., and so will your Royal Highness before six months are over." "No, no, I'll be damned if ever I do such an effeminate thing as that." Story of the P. Attempted once to shoot himself on account of Mrs Fitzherbert; only fired at the top of the bed, and then punctured himself with a sword in the breast. Lord E. thinks the Queen of France was innocent; so thought Lord Whitworth. If she erred with any one, it was Fersen, a Swede, he who assisted in her escape.

September 4 Lord H. told at breakfast of the old Lady Albemarle (I think) saying to some one, "You have heard that I have abused you, but it is not true, for I would not take the trouble of talking about you; but if I *had* said anything of you, it would have been that you look like a blackguard of week days, and on Sundays like an apothecary." Lord H. full of an epigram he had just written on Southey, which we all twisted and turned into various shapes, he as happy as a boy during the operation. It was thus at last:

> Omnibus hoc vitium est cantoribus.
> Our Laureat Bob defrauds the king,
> He takes his cash and does not sing:
> Yet on he goes, I know not why,
> Singing for us who do not buy.

In the evening, to my surprise and pleasure, Mrs Leigh[1] appeared. Could not help looking at her with deep interest; though she can hardly be said to be like Byron, yet she reminds one of him. Was still more pleased, when, evidently at her own request, Lady Stanhope introduced me to her: found her pleasing, though (as I had always heard) nothing above the ordinary run of women. She herself began first to talk of him, after some time, by asking me "whether I saw any likeness." I answered, I did; and she said it was with strong fears of being answered "No," that she had asked the question. Talked of different pictures of him. I felt it difficult to keep the tears out of my eyes as I spoke with her. Said she would show me the miniature which she thought the best, if I would call upon her.

October 16 A letter from the Longmans to say that they have sold every copy of the first 1000[2], and that the octavo will not be ready for two or three weeks. Take for granted, therefore, that there is a second quarto edition. Much inclined to give up my Paris trip for various reasons; the expense, Bessy's health, the idleness, and one or two more things.

October 17 Bessy would not hear of my staying at home: insisted that if I did not go to France, I must go either to Scotland or Ireland, to amuse myself a

---

[1] Byron's half-sister the Hon. Augusta Byron (1783–1851) and wife of Col. George Leigh. The poet was passionately fond of her, and it was hinted during his lifetime and is now fairly generally held, that he was her lover.
[2] Copies of Moore's *Life of Sheridan*.

little. Dear, generous girl, there never was anything like her for warm-heartedness and devotion. I shall certainly do no good at home, from the daily fidget I am kept in about my book. So perhaps an excursion somewhere, merely to change the current of my thoughts, would be of use.

October 29 Set off between eleven and twelve in a chaise for Sir Walter Scott's. Stopped on the way to see Dryburgh Abbey on the grounds of Lord Buchan. The vault of Sir Walter Scott's family is here. Lord Buchan's own tombstone, ready placed, with a Latin inscription by himself on it, and a cast from his face let into the stone. Forded the Tweed below the chain bridge, and passed through Melrose, having a peep at the Abbey on my way, but reserving my view of it till I could see it with Scott himself. Arrived at his house about two. His reception of me most hearty; we had met but once before, so long ago as immediately after his publication of the *Lay of the Last Minstrel*. After presenting me to Lady Scott and his daughter Anne (the Lockharts having, unluckily, just gone to Edinburgh), he and I started for a walk. Said how much he was delighted with Ireland; the fun of the common people. The postilion having run the pole against the corner of a wall and broken it down, crying out, "Well done pole! didn't the pole do it elegantly, your honour?" Pointing to the opposite bank of the river, said it was believed still by some of the common people that the fairies danced in that spot; and as a proof of it, mentioned a fellow having declared before him, in his judicial capacity, that having gone to pen his sheep about sunrise in a field two or three miles further down the river, he had seen little men and women under a hedge, beautifully dressed in green and gold; "the Duke of Buccleugh in full dress was nothing to them." "Did you, by the virtue of your oath, believe them to be fairies?" "I dinna ken; they looked very like the gude people" (evidently believing them to be fairies). The fact was, however, that these fairies were puppets belonging to an itinerant showman, which some weavers, in a drunken frolic, had taken a fancy to and robbed him of, but, fearing the consequences when sober, had thrown them under a hedge, where this fellow saw them...

When I remarked that every magazine now contained such poetry as would have made a reputation for a man some twenty or thirty years ago, he said (with much shrewd humour in his face), "Ecod, we were in the luck of it, to come before all this talent was at work." Agreed with me that it would be some time before a great literary reputation could be again called up, "unless (he added) something new could be struck out; everything that succeeded lately owing its success, in a great degree, to its novelty." Talked a good deal about Byron; thinks his last cantos of *Don Juan* the most powerful things he ever wrote. Talking of the report of Lady Byron being about to marry Cunningham, said he would not believe it. "No, no, she must never let another man bear the name of husband to her." In talking of my sacrifice of the "Memoirs," said he was well aware of the honourable feelings that dictated it,

but doubted whether he would himself have consented
to it. On my representing, however, the strong circumstances of not only the sister of Lord Byron (whom
he so much loved) requiring it, but his two most intimate
friends, Kinnaird and Hobhouse, also insisting earnestly
upon the total destruction of the MS., and the latter
assuring me that Lord Byron had expressed to him
regret for having put such a work out of his own power,
and had said that he was only restrained by delicacy
towards me from recalling it; when I mentioned these
circumstances (and particularly the last), he seemed to
feel I could not have done otherwise than I had done.
Thought the family, however, bound to furnish me
every assistance towards a life of Lord B. I spoke of
the advantage of Scotland over Ireland in her national
recollections, in which he agreed and remarked the good
luck of Scotland, in at last giving a king to England. In
the spirit of this superiority he had himself insisted, in
all the ceremonials attending the king's reception in
Scotland, that England should yield the precedence;
there had been some little tiffs about it, but the king
himself had agreed readily to everything proposed to
him. In talking of Ireland, said that he and Lockhart
had gone there rather hostilely disposed towards the
Catholic Emancipation, but that they had both returned
converts to the necessity of conceding it. Dined at half-
past five; none but himself, Mr George Huntly
Gordon[1], who is making a catalogue of his library,

[1] Scott's amanuensis, who was also at the time of Moore's
visit transcribing the first two volumes of the *Life of Napoleon*.
[Lord John Russell's Note.]

Lady Scott and daughter, and a boy, the son of his lost friend, William Erskine. After dinner pledged him in some whisky out of a *quaigh*; that which I drank out of very curious and beautiful. Produced several others; one that belonged to Prince Charles, with a glass bottom; others of a larger size, out of which he said his great grandfather drank. Very interesting *tête-à-tête* with him after dinner. Said that the person who first set him upon trying his talent at poetry was Mat. Lewis. He had passed the early part of his life with a set of clever, rattling, drinking fellows, whose thoughts and talents lay wholly out of the region of poetry; he, therefore, had never been led to find out his turn for it, though always fond of the old ballads. In the course of the conversation he, at last (to my no small surprise and pleasure), mentioned the novels without the least reserve as his own; "I then hit upon these novels (he said), which have been a mine of wealth to me." Had begun *Waverley* long before, and then thrown it by, till, having occasion for some money (to help his brother, I think), he bethought himself of it, but could not find the MS.; nor was it till he came to Abbotsford that he at last stumbled upon it. By this he made £3000. The conjectures and mystification at first amused him very much: wonders himself that the secret was so well kept, as about twenty persons knew it from the first. The story of Jeanie Deans founded upon an anonymous letter which he received; has never known from whom. The circumstance of the girl having refused the testimony in court, and then taking the journey to obtain her sister's pardon, is a fact. Received some hints also from Lady Louisa Stuart (granddaughter, I believe, to Lord Bute); these the only aids afforded to him. His only critic was the printer[1], who was in the secret, and who now and then started objections which he generally attended to. Had always been in the habit (while wandering alone or shooting) of forming stories and following a train of adventures in his mind, and these fancies it was that formed the groundwork of most of his novels. "I find I fail in them now, however (he said): I cannot make them as good as at first." He is now near fifty-seven; has no knowledge or feeling of music; knows nothing of Greek; indebted to Pope for even his knowledge of Homer. Spoke of the scrape he got into by the false quantity in his Latin epitaph on his dog. I said that his letter on the subject was worth all the prosody that ever existed, and so it is; nothing was ever in better or more manly taste. In the evening Miss Scott sung two old Scotch songs to the harp. He spoke of Mrs Lockhart (whom he seems thoroughly to love) as richer in this style of songs than Miss Scott. I then sung several things which he seemed to like. Spoke of my happy power of adapting words to music, which, he said, he could never attain, nor could Byron either. Story of the beggar: "Give that man some halfpence and send him away"; "I never go away under sixpence." Spoke of the powers of all Irishmen for oratory; the Scotch, on the contrary, cannot speak; no Scotch orator can be named; no Scotch actors. Told me Lockhart was about to undertake the *Quarterly*, has agreed for five years; salary £1200. a year, and if he

[1] James Ballantyne. [Lord John Russell's Note.]

writes a certain number of articles it will be £1500. a
year to him. Spoke of Wordsworth's absurd vanity about
his own poetry; the more remarkable as Wordsworth
seems otherwise a manly fellow. Story told him by
Wordsworth, of Sir George Beaumont saying one day
to Crabbe, at Murray's, on Crabbe putting an ex-
tinguisher on a tallow candle which had been imperfectly put out, and the smoke of which was (as Sir G.
Beaumont said) curling up in graceful wreaths, "What,
you a poet, and do that?" This Wordsworth told Scott
was a set-off against the latter's praises of Crabbe, and
as containing his own feelings on the subject, as well
as Sir G. Beaumont's. What wretched twaddle! Described Wordsworth's manly endurance of his poverty.
Scott has dined with him at that time in his kitchen;
but though a kitchen, all was neatness in it. Spoke of
Campbell; praised his *Hohenlinden*, &c.; considered his
Pleasures of Hope as very inferior to these lesser pieces.
Talked of Holt, the Wicklow brigand, who held out
so long in the mountains, and who distinguished himself
on many occasions by great generosity; once or twice
gave up men who had been guilty of acts of cruelty;
is still alive, keeping (I believe), a publichouse, and in
good repute for quietness. Sir Walter Scott had wished
much to have some talk with him, but feared it might
do the man harm, by giving him high notions of himself, &c. &c. "I could have put," says he, "a thousand
pounds in his pocket, by getting him to tell simply the
adventures in which he had been engaged, and then
dressing them up for him." In speaking of the circumstances in which my intimacy with Byron began, and

giving him an account of the message from Greville that followed, he spoke as if the thought had occurred to him at that time, whether he ought not himself to have taken notice, in the same manner, of what Byron had said of him.

October 30 A very stormy day. Sir W. impatient to take me out to walk, though the ladies said we should be sure of a ducking. At last a tolerably fair moment came, and we started; he would not take a great coat. Had explained to me after breakfast, the drawings in the breakfast room, done by an amateur at Edinburgh, W. Sharpe, and alluding to traditions of the Scotts of Harden, Sir Walter's ancestors. The subject of one of them was the circumstance of a young man of the family being taken prisoner in an incursion on the grounds of a neighbouring chief, who gave him his choice, whether he should be hanged or marry his daughter, "muckle-mouthed Meg." The sketch represents the young man as hesitating; a priest advising him to the marriage, and pointing to the gallows on a distant hill, while Meg herself is stretching her wide mouth in joyful anticipation of a decision in her favour. The other sketch is founded on the old custom of giving a hint to the guests that the last of the beeves has been devoured, by serving up nothing but a pair of spurs under one of the covers; the dismay of the party at the uncovering of the dish, is cleverly expressed. Our walk was to the cottage of W. Laidlaw[1], his bailiff, a

[1] William Laidlaw (1780–1845), a poet, author of the ballad *Lucy's Flittin'*.

man who had been reduced from better circumstances, and of whom Scott spoke with much respect as a person every way estimable. His intention was, he said, to ask him to walk down and dine with us to-day. The cottage, and the mistress of it very homely, but the man himself, with his broad Scotch dialect, showing the quiet self-possession of a man of good sense. The storm grew violent, and we sat some time. Scott said he could enumerate thirty places, famous in Scottish song, that could be pointed out from a hill in his neighbourhood: Yarrow, Ettrick, Gala Water, Bush-aboon Traquair, Selkirk ("Up with the souters of Selkirk"), the bonny Cowden Knowes, &c. &c. Mentioned that the Duke of Wellington had once wept, in speaking to him about Waterloo, saying that "the next dreadful thing to a battle lost was a battle won." Company to dinner, Sir Adam Ferguson (an old schoolfellow and friend of Scott), his lady, and Col. Ferguson. Drew out Sir Adam (as he had promised me he would) to tell some of his military stories, which were very amusing. Talked of amateurs in battles; the Duke of Richmond at Waterloo, &c. &c.; the little regard that is had of them. A story of one who had volunteered with a friend of his to the bombardment of Copenhagen, and after a severe cannonade, when a sergeant of marines came to report the loss, he said (after mentioning Jack This and Tom That, who had been killed), "Oh, please your Honour, I forgot to say that the volunteer gentleman has had his head shot off." Scott mentioned as a curious circumstance that, at the same moment, the Duke of Wellington should have been living in one of Buonaparte's palaces, and Buonaparte in the Duke's old lodgings at St Helena; had heard the Duke say laughingly to some one who asked what commands he had to St Helena, "Only tell Bony that I hope he finds my old lodgings at Longwood as comfortable as I find his in the Champs Elysées." Mentioned the story on which the Scotch song of *Dainty Davie*, was founded. Talking of ghosts, Sir Adam said that Scott and he had seen one, at least, while they were once drinking together; a very hideous fellow appeared suddenly between them whom neither knew anything about, but whom both saw. Scott did not deny it, but said they were both "fou," and not very capable of judging whether it was a ghost or not. Scott said that the only two men, who had ever told him that they had actually seen a ghost, afterwards put an end to themselves. One was Lord Castlereagh, who had himself mentioned to Scott his seeing the "radiant-boy." It was one night when he was in barracks, and the face brightened gradually out of the fireplace, and approached him. Lord Castlereagh stepped forwards to it, and it receded again, and faded into the same place. It is generally stated to have been an apparition attached to the family, and coming occasionally to presage honours and prosperity to him before whom it appeared, but Lord Castlereagh gave no such account of it to Scott. It was the Duke of Wellington made Lord Castlereagh tell the story to Sir Walter, and Lord C. told it without hesitation, and as if believing in it implicitly. Told of the Provost of Edinburgh showing the curiosities of that city to the Persian ambassador; impatience of the latter, and the stammering hesitation of the former.

"Many pillar, wood pillar? stone pillar, eh?" "Ba-ba-ba-ba," stammered the Provost. "Ah, you not know; var well. Many book here: write book? print book, eh?" "Ba-ba-ba-ba." "Ah, you not know; var well." A few days after, on seeing the Provost pass his lodgings, threw up the window and cried, "Ah, how you do?" "Ba-ba-ba." "Ah, you not know; var well"; and shut down the window. Account of the meeting between Adam Smith and Johnson as given by Smith himself. Johnson began by attacking Hume. "I saw (said Smith) this was meant at me, so I merely put him right as to a matter of fact." "Well, what did he say?" "He said it was a lie." "And what did you say to that?" "I told him he was a son of a b——h." Good this, between two sages. Boswell's father indignant at his son's attaching himself (as he said) to "a Dominie, who kippit a schule, and ca'd it an academy." Some doubts, after dinner, whether we should have any singing, it being Sunday. Miss Scott seemed to think the rule might be infringed in my case; but Scott settled the matter more decorously, by asking the Fergusons to come again to dinner next day, and to bring the Misses Ferguson.

October 31 Set off after breakfast, Scott, Miss Scott, and I, to go to Melrose Abbey. Told him I had had a strong idea of coming on as far as Melrose from Kelso on Friday night, in order to see the Abbey by the beautiful moonlight we had then; but that I thought it still better to reserve myself for the chance of seeing it with him, though I had heard he was not fond now of showing it. He answered, that in general he was not;

but that I was, of course, an exception. I think it was on this morning that he said, laying his hand cordially on my breast, "Now, my dear Moore, we are friends for life." Forgot to mention that, in the answer which he sent to me at Newcastle, and which was forwarded after me to Abbotsford, he offered, if I would let him know when I should reach Kelso, to come for me there in his carriage; nothing, indeed, could be more kind and cordial than the whole of his reception of me. Explained to me all the parts of the Abbey, assisted by the sexton, a shrewd, hardy-mannered fellow, who seemed to have studied everything relating to it *con amore*. Went up to a room in the sexton's house, which was filled with casts, done by himself, from the ornaments, heads, &c. of the Abbey. Scott, seeing a large niche empty, said, "Johnny, I'll give you the Virgin and Child to put there." Seldom have I seen a happier face than Johnny exhibited at this news; it was all over smiles. As we went downstairs, Scott said to him, "Johnny, if there's another anti-Popish rising, you'll have your house pulled about your ears." When we got into the carriage, I said, "You have made that man very happy." "Good (said Sir Walter), then there are two of us pleased, for I did not know what to do with the Virgin and Child. Mamma (Lady Scott) will be particularly glad to get rid of it." A less natural man would have left me under the impression that he had done really a very generous thing. Sir W. bought one of the books giving a description of the Abbey (written every word of it by the sexton), and presented it to me. Went from thence to the cottage of the Lockharts, which is very retired and pretty; and then proceeded to pay a visit to the Fergusons just near. Could not help thinking, during this quiet homely visit, how astonished some of those foreigners would be, to whom the name of Sir Walter Scott is encircled with so much romance, to see the plain, quiet, neighbourly manner with which he took his seat among these old maids, and the familiar ease with which they treated him in return; no country squire, with but half an idea in his head, could have fallen into the gossip of a humdrum country visit more unassumingly. This is charming. Left Miss Scott to proceed home in the carriage: and he and I walked. Took me through a wild and pretty glen called "Thomas the Rhymer's Glen." Told me of his introduction to the Prince by Adam; their whole talk about the Pretender. The Prince asked him, would he have joined the Jacobites; "It would have been wretched taste of me (said Scott) to have said I would, and I merely answered that I should have, at least, wanted one motive against doing so in not knowing his Royal Highness." Adam said afterwards, that the only difference as to Jacobitism between him and the Prince, during the conversation, was, that the Prince always said "The Pretender," and Scott said "Prince Charles." Mentioned that when Buonaparte expressed himself shocked at the murder of the Emperor Paul, Fouché said, "Mais, Sire, c'est une espèce de destitution propre à ce pays-là." On my taking this opportunity of saying that I doubted whether I ought to allude to a work which it was supposed he was writing, "The Life of Buonaparte," he said that it was true, and that he had already finished, I think, more than a volume of it, but had now suspended his task for the purpose of writing a novel on the subject of the "Civil Wars," in which he expected to make something of the character of Cromwell, whose politics he certainly did not like, but in whom there were some noble points which he should like to throw light on. It gave me pleasure to find that some of the views he expressed of the character of Napoleon were liberal; talked with scorn of the wretched attempts to decry his courage. I said how well calculated the way in which Scott had been brought up was to make a writer of poetry and romance, as it combined all that knowledge of rural life and rural legends which is to be gained by living among the peasantry and joining in their sports, with all the advantages which an aristocratic education gives. I said that the want of this manly training showed itself in my poetry, which would perhaps have had a far more vigorous character if it had not been for the sort of *boudoir* education I had received. (The only thing, indeed, that conduced to brace and invigorate my mind was the strong political feelings that were stirring around me when I was a boy, and in which I took a deep and most ardent interest.) Scott was good-natured enough to dissent from all this. His grandfather, he told me, had been, when a young man, very poor; and a shepherd, who had lived with the family, came and offered him the loan of (I believe all the money he had) thirty pounds, for the purpose of stocking a farm with sheep. The grandfather accepted it, and went to the fair, but instead of buying the sheep, he laid out the whole sum on a

horse, much to the horror of the poor shepherd. Having got the horse, however, into good training and order, he appeared on him at a hunt, and showed him off in such style, that he immediately found a purchaser for him at twice the sum he cost him, and then, having paid the shepherd his £30., he laid out the remainder in sheep, and prospered considerably. Pointed out to me the tower where he was born. His father and uncle went off to join the rebels in 1745, but were brought back; himself still a sort of Jacobite; has a feeling of horror at the very name of the Duke of Cumberland.
..... Came to a pretty lake where he fed a large beautiful swan, that seemed an old favourite of his. The Fergusons to dinner; maiden sisters and all. Showed me before dinner, in a printed song book, a very pretty ballad by his bailiff, Mr Laidlaw, called *Lucy's Flitting*. In the evening I sung, and all seemed very much pleased; Sir Adam, too, and his brother the Colonel, sung. Scott confessed that he hardly knew high from low in music. Told him Lord Byron knew nothing of music, but still had a strong feeling of some of those I had just sung, particularly *When he who adores thee*; that I have sometimes seen the tears come into his eyes at some of my songs. Another great favourite of his was *Though the last glimpse of Erin*, from which he confessedly borrowed a thought for his *Corsair*, and said to me, "It was shabby of me, Tom, not to acknowledge that theft." "I dare say," said Scott, "Byron's feelings and mine about music are pretty much the same." His true delight, however, was visible after supper, when Sir Adam sung some old Jacobite songs;

Scott's eyes sparkled, and his attempts to join in chorus showed much more of the will than the deed. *Hey, tutti tutte*, was sung in the true orthodox manner, all of us standing round the table with hands crossed and joined, and chorusing every verse with all our might and main; he seemed to enjoy all this thoroughly. Asked him this morning whether he was not a great admirer of Bruce the traveller; said he was his delight; and I could have sworn so.

November 1 Scott proposed to take me to-day to the castle of Newark, a place of the Duke of Buccleugh's. Sat with him some time in his study: saw a copy of the *Moniteur* there, which he said he meant to give to the Advocates' Library when he was done with it. I said that what astonished foreigners most was the extent of his knowledge. "Ah, that sort of knowledge (he answered) is very superficial." I remarked that the manual labour alone of copying out his works seemed enough to have occupied all the time he had taken in producing them. "I write," he answered, "very quick; that comes of being brought up under an attorney." Writes chiefly in the morning, from seven till breakfast time: told me the number of pages he could generally produce in the day, but I do not accurately remember how much it was. Mentioned to him that Lord Byron repeated to me the first hundred and twenty lines of *Lara* immediately after they were written, and said he had done them either that morning or the evening before, I forgot which. Went out at twelve in the open carriage, he and I and Miss Scott; the day very lowering.

Showed me where the Ettrick and Yarrow join. The Yarrow grows beautiful near the gate of the Duke, and the walk by it through the grounds is charming. Lunched in a little summer-house beyond the bridge. Showed me a deep part of the river into which he found Mungo Park once throwing stones: Park said it reminded him of what he used to do in Africa to try the depth of the rivers. After his return from Africa he opened an apothecary's shop in Selkirk, but the passion for wandering would not allow him to remain quiet. Day cleared up as we returned home. Saw the place where Montrose was defeated; four hundred Irishmen shot near it after the battle. In talking of his ignorance of music, Scott said he had been once employed in a case where a purchaser of a fiddle had been imposed upon as to its value. He found it necessary to prepare himself by reading all about fiddles in the Encyclopædias, &c., and having got the names of Straduerius, Amati, &c. glibly on his tongue, got swimmingly through his cause. Not long after this, dining at the Duke of Hamilton's, he found himself left alone after dinner with the Duke, who had but two subjects he could talk of, hunting and music. Having exhausted hunting, Scott thought he would bring forward his lately acquired learning in fiddles; upon which the Duke grew quite animated, and immediately whispered some orders to the butler, in consequence of which there soon entered the room about half a dozen tall servants all in red, each bearing a fiddle case; and Scott found his knowledge brought to no less a test than that of telling by the tones of each fiddle, as the Duke played it, by what artist it was made. "By guessing and management," he said, "I got on pretty well till we were, to my great relief, summoned to coffee." Mentioned an anecdote which he had heard from Lady Swinton of her seeing, when a child, a strange young lady in the room whom she took for a spirit, from her vanishing the moment she turned her head. It was a person whom her mother kept concealed, from some cause, within the panel: this evidently suggested the circumstance in one of his novels. On our return home found that two gentlemen were waiting to see Sir Walter; proved to be young Demidoff, son of the rich Russian, who has been sent to Edinburgh for his education, and with his tutor, was now come to pay a visit to Sir Walter[1]. Much talk with the young man, who is very intelligent, about Russian literature. I mentioned the *Fables* of Kriloff, of which I had seen a translation in French, and in one of which he talks of Voltaire being roasted in hell *à petit feu*. This translation, Demidoff said, was a very bad one. Sung in the evening; much pressed by Scott to defer my departure for a day or two.

November 2 While I was dressing, Mr Gordon (the gentleman who is employed making a catalogue of the library) came into my room, and requested, as a great favour, a lock of my hair: told him to be careful how he cut it, as Mrs Moore would be sure to detect the

[1] A gentleman who was at Abbotsford at the time, declares that it was Count Orloff, a nephew of the Count Orloff who holds a high station at the Russian Court, who was Sir Walter Scott's guest, and not M. Demidoff. [Lord John Russell's Note.]

"rape." The carriage being ordered immediately after breakfast, to take me to the coach and young Demidoff and his tutor to Melrose Abbey, I took leave of Scott, who seemed (as my companions afterwards remarked) to feel much regret at parting with me. Finding a place in the Jedburgh coach, I set off for Edinburgh. Some talk among the people in the coach about Scott; said he was "a very peculiar man," and seemed all to agree that he had chosen a very bad situation for his house. Went outside for the last two or three stages, in order to see the country, but it was all dreary and barren. The entrance, however, into Edinburgh most striking; the deep ravine between the two towns, the picturesque sites of the buildings on the heights and in the depths, the grand openings to the sea, all is magnificent and unlike everything else. By the bye, talking with the guard about Abbotsford, he told me Lady Scott had said that "it was quite an hotel in everything but pay." Took a hackney coach and drove to William Murray's (husband to Bessy's sister), having received a letter from him at Abbotsford, entreating me to take a bed at his house. Found Anne not so much altered (though it is fourteen years since we last met) as Bessy led me to expect. A note while we were at dinner from Murray's sister, Mrs Siddons, to ask me, if not too fatigued, to drink tea there. We went; none but herself and daughters; sung a little, though very hoarse; one of the Miss S.'s also sung. Had written to Jeffrey after dinner to say I was come, and would be out with him at Craigcrook to-morrow; an answer from him to say, "Why not to-night?"

November 5 After breakfast, young Stoddart (grandson to Sir H. Moncrieff) came out to beg I would fix a day to dine with Sir Henry; fixed for next Tuesday. Set off to walk to town, but, near the house, met the "Man of Feeling" coming out to call upon me. Jeffrey put me into the carriage to him, and he carried me into town. Told me that what put him upon writing *Julia de Roubigny*, was a wish expressed by Lord Kaimes for a novel without love in it. Dosed me with old stories and civility; and having stopped his carriage half way down a hill, in order to introduce me to his daughter, who was coming up it, left me at last at Murray's house. Walked out with Murray, and went to see Holyrood House: felt, as I looked at the wretched lodgings around it for the privileged, how much better I had been within the rules of the Allée des Veuves, in 1820. Dined at Mrs Siddons's, with Murray and Anne: company, the Lord Provost, Shannon, &c. &c. A party in the evening: Miss Gibson Craig, a pretty girl; two other nice girls, Miss Wilsons, very good musicians, rather a rare thing, it appears, in Scotland. Sung with them some Italian duets and trios: one of them sung my own *Say what shall be our sport to-day?* The evening agreeable.

November 6 Went off with Murray, in a hackney-coach to see Roslyn Castle; the day clear and sunny, and, considering the time of the year, very favourable for the purpose. The colouring of the leaves, rocks, and water brought out beautifully by the sunshine. Did not go on to Hawthornden: the chapel very curious.

Lunched at the inn, well and cheaply. Company to dinner at Murray's, John Wilson[1], the professor of Moral Philosophy (author of the novels, *Blackwood*, &c.), Ballantyne the printer (Scott's friend, and, as Scott told me, the only critic he had for his novels), and Shannon. Wilson an odd person, but amusing; his imitation of Wordsworth's Monologues excellent. Spoke of my "Sheridan"; thinks the *bon mots* I have reported of his very poor; told him I agreed with him in this, but was obliged to put them in, both from the outcry there would have been, had I not given anecdotes, and the value in which most of those I have given are held by Rogers, Lord Holland, &c., particularly the reply to Tarleton about the mule and the ass, which I saw no great merit in myself, but which Lord H. and Rogers always quote with praise. All agreed in thinking it not only poor, but hardly intelligible. Wilson praised my book warmly, and said that it was only so far unfair that the biographer had in every page outshone his subject. Seemed not to think very highly of Sheridan's genius; and in speaking of his great unreported speech, said it appeared to him utterly impossible that, with such powers as his, he should ever have produced anything deserving of such high praises. In comparing prose with poetry, remarked, in order to prove the inferiority of the former, that there have been great schools of poetry, but no school of prose. Sat drinking till rather late, and sat again with Wilson after supper, till past one. Not being able to dine with him any

---

[1] John Wilson (1785–1854), essayist and critic, the famous "Christopher North" of *Blackwood's Magazine*.

day before I go, fixed to sup at his house next Tuesday.

November 8 Company to breakfast, Capt. Basil Hall and his wife, old Mackenzie, &c. &c. Sung for them after breakfast. Have more than once seen Jeffrey (though he professes rather to dislike music) with tears in his eyes while I sang *There's a Song of the Olden Time*, one of those that make the most impression. John A. Murray, having sent out his gig for me, I took leave of Craigcrook, leaving, I hope, as pleasant recollections of my visit as I brought away with me. Letters from Mrs Dugald Stewart and old Mr Fletcher (a friend of Mackintosh's), full of the most flattering kindness. Mrs Stewart says that her husband would have come to Edinburgh to meet me, if it was not for the bad weather, and Mr Fletcher, with many praises of my writings, expresses his regret that his infirmities would not allow him to do the same: both invite me to their houses. Took my place in the mail for Thursday morning. Dined at Sir Henry Moncrieff's: company, Jeffrey, J. A. Murray, Dr Thomson, young Stoddart and his sister, and one or two more. Sung to a wretched pianoforte in the evening. Went from thence to Miss Sinclair's; with W. Murray's assistance escaped early, and he and I went to sup at Wilson's. An odd set collected there; among others the poet Hogg. We had also Williams, the Rector of the Academy, the person to whom Lockhart addressed *Peter's Letters*; said to be an able man; some ladies too, one of whom sung duets with an Italian singing-master: a fine contrast between this foreigner and Hogg, who yelled out savagely two or three Scotch songs, and accompanied the burden of one of them by labouring away upon the bare shoulders of the ladies who sat on each side of him. He and I very cordial together; wanted me to let him drive me to his farm next day, to see wife and bairns. I was much pressed to sing, but there being no pianoforte could not; at last, in order not to seem fine (the great difficulty one has to get over in such society), sung the *Boys of Kilkenny*.

November 12 Went to the Courts after breakfast: found out Jeffrey and walked about with him to see everything, being myself the greatest show of the place and followed by crowds from court to court. Had the pleasure of seeing Scott sitting at his table, under a row of as dull-looking judges as need be. Jeffrey asked him to dine to meet me, and though I had already refused Jeffrey (in order to dine with the Murrays), I could not resist this temptation: begged of Jeffrey to dine pretty early, in order that I might see the theatre. Met Scott afterwards, and told him this arrangement. "Very well," he said, "I'll order my carriage to come at eight o'clock, and I'll just step down to the playhouse with you myself." Company at Jeffrey's, Mr and Mrs Rutherford, Thomson, &c. Sir Walter a different man from what he was at Abbotsford; a good deal more inert, and, when he did come into play, not near so engaging or amusing. When the carriage came, he and I and Thomson went to the theatre, and I could see that Scott anticipated the sort of reception I met with. We went into the front boxes, and the moment we appeared, the whole pit rose, turned towards us, and applauded vehemently. Scott said, "It is you, it is you; you must rise and make your acknowledgment." I hesitated for some time, but on hearing them shout out "Moore, Moore," I rose and bowed my best for two or three minutes. This scene was repeated after the two next acts, and the *Irish Melodies* were played each time by the orchestra. Soon after my first reception, Jeffrey and two of the ladies arrived, and sat in the front before us, Scott and I being in the second row. He seemed highly pleased the way I was received, and said several times, "This is quite right. I am glad my countrymen have returned the compliment for me." There was occasionally some discontent expressed by the galleries at our being placed where they could not see us; and Murray told me afterwards, that he wondered they bore it so well. We had taken the precaution of ordering that we should be shown into one of the side boxes, but the proper box-keeper was out of the way when we came. At about ten o'clock we came away, I having first renewed my acquaintance with Mrs Coutts, who was with the Duke of St Albans in a box near us. Home very tired with my glory, and had to pack for the morning.

December 11 Received two letters (one of which I ought to have got yesterday) from my sister Ellen, telling me that my dear father is dangerously ill: the event I have been but too well prepared for. God send he may not have pain or lingering. His long life has been one of almost uninterrupted health, and I have been able (thank Heaven!) to make his latter days tranquil and comfortable. It is my poor mother I have now most to feel for. Must start immediately for Ireland, but this being Sunday can make no arrangements for money. The shock at first very great, notwithstanding the prepared state of my feelings; darling Bessy full of the sweetest sympathy and kindness about it. Wrote to Corry, to say I trusted in his friendship for everything being done that ought to be done, and begging him to communicate to Ellen my intention to set off immediately.

December 12 ... Dined at three, and set off at five in a chaise for Bath. Went, on my arrival, to see Anastasia: found the sweet child in the midst of gaiety: it was the ball night, and she came out to me, "smiling, as if earth contained no tomb." On my telling her of the sad mission I was going upon, she assumed that grave look which children think it right to put on at such news, though they cannot be expected, and, indeed, *ought* not to feel it. She wore three or four orders of merit which she had gained; one, for general amiability of conduct (a lily of the valley), of which she told me with much triumph, there had been but four given in the school; another (a rose) for her progress in music, and so on. Slept at the York House: got them to give me a letter to the landlord of the inn at Birmingham to secure me a comfortable bed. Found in the coffee-room an old acquaintance (Birmingham, the clergyman), with two sons of Charles Butler, on their way to Ireland.

December 14 There being so many candidates for the coach at the Albion, went to the Swan, to take my chance in the mail: got a place; my companions, a dull good-natured Scotchman, and a young lady with a little girl under her charge, who left us at Shrewsbury. Took in a gentleman as far as Oswestry, who proved to be a merchant of some kind at Liverpool: some interesting conversation on commercial matters. Liverpool and Manchester have been wise enough to keep clear of local notes; many attempts made to introduce them, but all resisted. In one stage between Llangollen and Corwen, there came on the most dreadful storm of thunder, lightning, and hail that ever I witnessed; the horses, though alarmed, behaved, luckily, very steadily; but the universal blazing of the sky and the pitch darkness that succeeded, the storm of hail blowing in the coachman's face, the horses in full career, and the guard crying out from behind, with evidently an alarmed voice, "Hold hard! hold hard!" were altogether circumstances by no means agreeable. Confess I felt a little frightened, and arranged myself on my seat in the safest attitude for an overset. Got safe, however, to Corwen; the coachman owned he was once very nearly off the road. At Bangor (where we arrived between one and two) resolved, as it would be so miserably wet and dark in crossing the ferry, to stop at Jackson's, and pass the day of rest I meant to give myself *there*, instead of at Holyhead. Had to knock the people up, and got to bed about three.

December 16 Up at five, and aboard the packet (Skinner's) at half-past six. Got into my berth immediately, where I lay without moving for the twelve long hours of our passage: by this means kept off actual sickness, but became even more deadly ill than if I had been sick. Overheard a man say to the under-steward in the cabin, "Isn't Mr Moore among the passengers?" "I don't know indeed, sir," was the answer. "His father (said the other) is——" (I didn't hear the word). "Is he?" said the steward. This appeared to me conclusive that all was over; and it is a proof of the power of the mind over even sea sickness, that though I was just then on the point of being sick, the dread certainty which these words conveyed to me quite checked the impulse, and I remained for some time even without a qualm. Did not stir till all the passengers had gone off by the coach, and then had a chaise and drove to M'Dowell's, in order to get something to eat, not having tasted food for twenty-eight hours. Found there Corry's two nephews; as they had only an open car to take them to Dublin, offered them seats in my chaise, and put my luggage into their car. Drove to Corry's and sent in for him; told me my father was still alive, but that was all. Went with me to Bilson's hotel, where he had got a bedroom for me. Assured me that I need not agitate myself as I did, for that my father was closing his eyes on the world without any suffering, and that my mother had already brought her mind to as much composure as could possibly be expected. Undertook to go and consult my sister Ellen, as to whether it would be too much for my mother to see me to-night; returned to say that I must come to her by all means, as she was expecting me, and it would be (Ellen thought) of the greatest service to her. Was glad to find from him that it was their strong wish I should not ask to see my father, as he was past the power of knowing me, and it would only shock me unnecessarily. This a great relief, as I would not for worlds have the sweet impression he left upon my mind when I last saw him exchanged for one which would haunt me, I know, dreadfully through the remainder of my life. It was Bessy's last wish that I should not arrive in time to see him alive, and her earnest request that I should not look on him afterwards. She knows how it would affect me. The meeting with my dearest mother, after the first burst, not so painful as I expected, and I soon found I could divert her mind to other subjects. My sister Kate had come up on the first alarm of his illness, and had taken her turn with Ellen in nursing and watching him ever since. Left them for my hotel between eleven and twelve, and had a much better night than I should have had, if I had remained in ignorance of my mother's mind. At parting, Ellen bid me not come too early in the morning, and said she would write me a note.

December 17 Took my time at breakfast, and waited for Ellen's note, but none came. Walked down to Abbey Street, and found that all was over; my dear father had died at seven in the morning. Consulted about the funeral, which it was the wish of all to have as simple and private as possible: entrusted the management of it to Mr Legh, the son of an old friend of my mother. Dined at Abbot's, and returned to my mother in the evening. Our conversation deeply interesting:

found that neither my mother nor Kate were very anxious to press upon him the presence of a clergyman; but on mentioning it to him at Corry's suggestion, he himself expressed a wish for it. The subject of religion was, indeed, the only one, it seems, upon which his mind was not gone. When the priest was proceeding to take his confession, and put the necessary questions for that purpose to him, he called my mother, and said, "Auty, my dear, you can tell this gentleman all he requires to know quite as well as I." This was very true, as she knew his every action and thought, and is a most touching trait of him. A few nights before he died, when Ellen was doing something for him, he said to her, "You are a valuable little girl, it's a pity some good man does not know your value." The apothecary, who was standing by, said with a smile, "Oh, sir, some good man *will*." "Not an apothecary, though," answered my father, which looked as if the playfulness, for which he was always so remarkable, had not even then deserted him. Our conversation naturally turned upon religion, and my sister Kate, who, the last time I saw her, was more than half inclined to declare herself a Protestant, told me she had since taken my advice and remained quietly a Catholic..... For myself, my having married a Protestant wife gave me an opportunity of choosing a religion, at least for my children, and if my marriage had no other advantage, I should think *this* quite sufficient to be grateful for. We then talked of the differences between the two faiths, and they who accuse all Catholics of being intolerantly attached to their own, would be either ashamed or surprised (according as they were sincere or not in the accusation) if they had heard the sentiments expressed both by my mother and sisters on the subject. Was glad to find I could divert my mother's mind from dwelling entirely on what had just happened; indeed, the natural buoyancy and excursiveness of her thoughts (which, luckily for myself, I have inherited) afforded a better chance of escape from grief than all the philosophy in the world. Left them late after fixing everything for Monday.

December 20 Had some talk with my sister Kate, as to what is to be done for my mother.... There was my admirable Bessy, before I left home, planning how *we* might contrive to do with but one servant, in order that I might be the better able to assist my mother.

February 10 *and* 11 Received through the Longmans all Scott's works, the joint present of Sir W. himself and Constable, with a very kind note from the latter. Fear that poor Scott's share in the ruin of Constable's house is even greater than I had supposed. Few things have affected me more than this. I almost regret, indeed, having been brought so close to Scott, as I might otherwise have been saved the deep and painful sympathy I now feel for his misfortune. For poor devils like me (who have never known better) to fag and to be pinched for means, becomes, as it were, a second nature; but for Scott, whom I saw living in such luxurious comfort, and dispensing such cordial hospitality, to be thus suddenly reduced to the *necessity* of working his way, is too bad, and I grieve for him from my heart.

May 11 Went with Benett to Deville's, in the Strand, the phrenologist and collector of casts; called for Sir Francis Burdett on our way at Brookes's. After having explained to us the principles of the science, he proceeded to examine our heads. Had some suspicion who Burdett was, but did not know me in the least. Found no poetry in my head, but a great love of facts and clearness in argument; humour, love of music, strong feelings of friendship (this Spurzheim too, I remember, remarked when I met him at Paris), a facility in parting with money, and "not being very particular as to the securities" (his very words, which amused the standers-by not a little), and the organs of combativeness and destructiveness as strong as ever he had witnessed them in any one. On Benett's asking him, whether he discovered in my head any particular talent, said, that he had seldom seen a head with "so active and general an organisation," and that whatever the person possessing it attempted, he would most probably succeed in. Told Burdett some things which he seemed to think true; among others, that his first perceptions of subjects were slow and rather confused, and that it was not till after some consideration he mastered and saw his way through them. A sense of justice and impatience under oppression was one of the features of Burdett's head, which he found also in mine. Went all together to the Exhibition. Burdett's criticism on Lawrence's picture of Canning, that it is "like an actor standing before a glass rehearsing his part," rather just.

May 14 Have exchanged visits and some notes with Hobhouse, but did not see him till to-day. Found him full of kindness, and inclined much more to assist than to thwart me in my design of writing "Byron's Life." Mentioned Byron's letters to Lady Melbourne, which Lady Cowper has still in her possession, and which he thinks more likely to contain passages fit to be extracted than any other of B.'s correspondence. Disclaimed ever having had the idea of writing the "Life" himself; thinks there are no materials to make a Life, which I fear is but too true. Dined at Chantrey's; had been engaged to Fielding's, but was let off on a promise of going early in the evening. Company, Henry Joy, a Mr Thompson, and two others. Talked of phrenology; Spurzheim's mistake at Chantrey's, in pronouncing Troughton[1] from his skull to be a poet, and Sir Walter Scott a mathematician. Chantrey at first inclined to believe in the science, but from seeing, from his experience, that there were clever heads of all sizes and shapes, lost his faith in it. An intimation of phrenology in Shakspeare's "foreheads villainously low."

May 27 Breakfasted at Rogers's; Sydney Smith, Lord Cawdor, G. Fortescue, and Warburton. Smith full of comicality and fancy; kept us all in roars of laughter. In talking of the stories about dram-drinkers catching fire, pursued the idea in every possible shape. The inconvenience of a man coming too near the candle when he was speaking, "Sir, your observation has caught fire." Then imagined a parson breaking into a blaze in the pulpit; the engines called to put him out; no water

---

[1] The well-known maker of philosophical instruments: himself a mathematician of high order. [Lord John Russell's Note.]

to be had, the man at the waterworks being an Unitarian or an Atheist. Left Rogers's with Smith, to go and assist him in choosing a grand pianoforte: found him (as I have often done before) change at once from the gay, uproarious way, into as solemn, grave, and austere a person as any bench of judges or bishops could supply: this I rather think his natural character. Called with him at Newton's to see my picture: said, in his gravest manner to Newton, "Couldn't you contrive to throw into his face somewhat a stronger expression of hostility to the Church establishment?"

October 21 Breakfasted with Rogers. Told me that after having called once or twice upon Murray without seeing him, he met him a day or two since at Lockhart's; when Murray himself opened upon the subject, and explained the meaning of his announcement by saying that the papers of Lord Byron in his hands had proved so abundant and curious that some friends had advised him to publish them first separately; and then (he added) Mr Moore is welcome to make all the use of them afterwards that he pleases. R. has been with Southey this summer. S.'s bigoted opinions; Charles I, he says, had but one fault, that of betraying his friend! his admiration of Laud, and his anger against Lord Holland for having called him "that bad man," in one of his speeches. "Only for my knowing Lord Holland (said Southey) I would have twigged him for that"; as if he considered himself the grand protector of all tyrants and bigots, living and dead. A witticism of Foote's: "Why are you for ever humming that air?" "Because it haunts me." "No wonder, for you are for ever *murdering* it." Told him of the state of my affairs with the Longmans, and of the offer I had made to settle with them; on which he very kindly said, "Why not settle with them at once? Lord Lansdowne would, I am sure, lend you a thousand guineas, and I'll lend you another thousand." When I was parting with him, having owned that I sometimes felt fits of despondency at the prospect before me, he said, "No, no, you have a noble spirit of your own, and you must keep it up, you dog." Altogether my conversation with him was very cheering to me. Called upon Luttrell, who walked with me to Power's and to Longman's. Told the Longmans of Murray's explanation of his announcement to Rogers. They read us some correspondence that had passed between them and him on the subject of Mrs Rundell's *Cookery*, from which we learned the curious fact that, after this book had for many years produced Murray seven or eight hundred a year, £2000. was given by him for the copyright of it. "Gad! one wonders (said Luttrell) that there should be *any* bad dinners going." Called at Pickering's in Chancery Lane, who showed us the original agreement between Milton and Symonds for the payment of five pounds for *Paradise Lost*. The contrast of this sum with the £2000. given for Mrs Rundell's *Cookery*, comprises a history in itself. Pickering, too, gave forty-five guineas for this agreement, three times as much as the whole sum given for the poem. It was part payment, I think (?). Went to Lawrence's: always wish I could like the man as much as I admire his works; but (as Luttrell says) "he is oily, and the oil bad into the bargain." Left my name at Lockhart's for Sir Walter Scott, who dined with the King at Windsor yesterday and had not yet returned.

October 22 ... Went to Scott's in the evening. Sir T. Lawrence having begged me to mention that *he* was within call, did so, and a note was immediately written to him, by Lockhart, to ask him. Scott mentioned the contrast in the behaviour of two criminals, whom he had himself seen: the one a woman, who had poisoned her husband in some drink, which she gave him while he was ill; the man not having the least suspicion, but leaning his head on her lap, while she still mixed more poison in the drink, as he became thirsty and asked for it. The other a man, who had made a bargain to sell a *subject* (a young child) to a surgeon; his bringing it at night in a bag; the surgeon's surprise at hearing it cry out; the man then saying, "Oh, you wanted it dead, did you?" and stepping behind a tree and killing it. The woman (who was brought up to judgment with a child at her breast) stood with the utmost calmness to hear her sentence; while the man, on the contrary, yelled out, and showed the most disgusting cowardice. Scott added, that this suggested to him the scene in *Marmion*. Sat down to a hot supper, of which Scott partook, and drank bottled porter; both myself and T. Lawrence following his example; then came the hot water and whiskey, in which we all joined also. This seems to be Scott's habitual practice. He spoke a good deal about Coleridge and Hogg, and recited, or rather tried to recite, some verses of the latter; but his memory appeared to me more wandering and imperfect than formerly.

October 23 Breakfasted at Scott's: Rogers there, and another person, whose name I did not make out. Talking of practical jokes, Rogers's story of somebody who, when tipsy, was first rolled in currant jelly, and then covered with feathers; his exclaiming, when he looked at himself in a glass, "A bird, by Jove!" Scott's story of the man whom they persuaded that the place he was walking in was full of adders; his fancying he felt an adder in his foot, and striking his foot violently with his stick, in order to kill it; hearing a hiss from out the boot, and then (as Scott said) "pelting away" at it again with his stick. "Ah, now he is silent, I think I have done for him"; then taking off his boot, and finding that it was his watch which had slipped down there, and which he had been thus hammering away at, the hiss having been the sound of the spring breaking. Scott's acting of this story admirable. In talking of their approaching trip to Paris I said, "How I should like to go with you"; upon which both he and Miss Scott caught eagerly at my words, and with an earnestness that was evidently *real*, pressed me to accompany them. Nothing could be more tempting, and I almost made up my mind to do it. Their departure fixed for Thursday; promised to let them know for a certainty on Wednesday. Scott said, as I was coming away, "Now, my dear Moore, do think seriously of this; you would be of the greatest service to me, and we have a place for you in the carriage; only you must take care and not rumple Anne's frills." Set off, with Rogers, for Murray's.

Talked, as we went, of my scheme of going with Scott. Threw a little *blight* over it; said it was an extraordinary frisk, but that it was like me; nobody else would think of it; that it never would surprise him (even after hearing me complain, as I did eternally, of pressure of business and want of time), to be told of my having set off on a party of pleasure *anywhere*, with *anybody*. He went into Murray's, while I walked about Albemarle Street. After a short interval came out for me, and he and I joined Murray in his office. Murray then repeated to me what he had just said to R., that his *only* reason for announcing the "Papers of Lord Byron" separate from the "Life," was to give a sort of *éclat* to his list of publications, and that he had not the least intention of departing from the plan which he, and I, and Hobhouse had agreed upon for the work in my last. Went to the Longmans to tell them of my idea of going with Scott; Longman highly pleased at the plan. Told him I should give Scott till to-morrow to consider of it, as there was certainly some degree of courage (standing in such high favour as he does with the King) in choosing a political reprobate like me for his companion. Longman said, Scott was not a man likely to have any fears or scruples of this kind. "Not if left to himself, probably; but he will meet shabby people enough to put it into his head, and, at all events, I will wait the chance of his changing his mind before I determine." Dined with Rogers at five. Quoted a good parody of Luttrell's written during the famine and brown-loaf time:

> Deepens the curses of each hungry oaf,
> And breathes a browner horror o'er the loaf.

October 24 On my way to breakfast with Newton called at Sir Walter's; a party with him at breakfast; not a word said by either himself or Miss Scott about my going with them to Paris. Felt how right I was in concluding that, upon reflection (or rather upon the representations of others), he would grow less eager on the subject. Richardson and Dr Holland among his guests at breakfast. Sat to Newton. After leaving him, in passing through Pall Mall, met Scott. "Well," he said, "it's all fixed; I have sent for your passport." "Do you really mean," I asked, "that I am to go with you?" "Most certainly," he answered; "I have quite set my heart on it." He then said, that he did not mean to stay more than seven days in Paris; that he would refuse all dinner engagements, &c. In talking of going from the Tower (which is the way he has fixed upon) said, "and we shall eat such a hearty dinner when we arrive at Calais!"...

To dinner at Lockhart's at five. Scott and Lockhart stood by while we were dining, as they were engaged to Wilmot Horton's dinner. All evidently bent on my joining them in their journey. Said I should be able to give them a decisive answer to-morrow; but that, at all events, it would not, I feared, be in my power to start with them on Thursday morning, but my intention was, if I went, to follow by the mail on Thursday night, and catch them at Calais, or a stage or two farther. Went to the play (to Mrs Coutt's box) with Mrs Lockhart, Miss Scott and Capt. Lockhart. In talking of her father's plans of retrenchment, Miss Scott said "Papa is a bad hand at economising"; and then added, laughing,

"All his great plans of retrenchment have ended in selling my horse!" The play, *Peveril of the Peak*, the third or fourth night. In trying to make out the plot Miss Scott said, "One confuses the stories of those novels, there are so many of them; 'pon my word, papa must write no more;" a proof that the mask is about to be thrown off entirely.

October 25 Breakfasted at the Athenæum. Received, while there, Bessy's answer to my letter; leaves me wholly to my own decision with respect to the trip to Paris. Almost made up my mind to go, but still had a feeling that I *should not*; the idea of taking advantage of Scott's *bonhomie*, and letting him do what he might afterwards repent of, hung about me still. Resolved, however, to make an effort to start *with* him from the Tower, and, if I could not manage that, not to go at all. Called upon Scott on my way home; told him I meant to make an effort to start with him from the Tower in the morning. He said, "That's right; but what will you do about your passport?" He then expressed his regret at not having my name put down in his, but asked did I not think I might, by taking a hackney coach and driving to Portland Place, prevail upon the secretary there (though it was now past the hour of business) to give me a passport. After some more conversation on the subject, left him. Made up my mind to give up the journey; whether it was fancy or not, thought I had seen a *little* change in Scott's manner on the subject; a slight abatement of his former eagerness for my going.

December 1 *to* 9 The letter from Orme, of the 5th, contained a proposal to me to become editor of an annual work which they meditate, on the plan of the *Forget-me-not, Souvenir,* &c. Speaks sanguinely of the prospect of its success, and says, if it turns out as they expect, it would give me an annual income of from five hundred to a thousand a year.

December 26 Gave a gay dinner, dancing, and supper to the servants in honour of Christmas.

December 30 Okeden mentioned having seen Lord Byron in a state of great excitement. On one occasion he made an effort to restrain himself, and succeeded; on the other, he gave full vent to his violence. The former was at Copet; when, on coming to dinner, he saw unexpectedly among the guests Mrs Harvey (Beckford's sister), whom he had not seen since the period of his marriage, and who was the person chiefly consulted by Lady Byron, I believe, on the subject of his proposals to her. He stopped short upon seeing her, turned deadly pale, and then clenching his hand, as if with a violent effort of self-restraint, resumed his usual manner. The other occasion was at Milan, when he and Hobhouse were ordered to quit the city in twenty-four hours, in consequence of a scrape which Polidori had brought them into the night before at the Opera, by desiring an officer, who sat before them, to take off his cap, and on his refusal to do so, attempting to take it off himself. The officer, upon this, coolly desired Polidori to follow him into the street, and the other two followed, ripe for a duel. The officer, however, assured them he had no such thing in his contemplation; that he was the officer of the guard for the night; and that, as to taking off his cap, it was contrary to orders, and he might lose his commission by doing so. Another part of his duty was to carry off Polidori to the guardhouse, which he accordingly did, and required the attendance of Byron and Hobhouse in the morning. The consequence of all this was, that the three were obliged to leave Milan immediately, Polidori having, in addition to this punishment, "bad conduct" assigned as the reason of his dismissal. It was in a few minutes after their receiving this notification that Okeden found Lord B. storming about the room, and Hobhouse after him, vainly endeavouring to tranquillise his temper. Must ask Hobhouse about this.

January 5 George Selwyn's criticism on Burke's *Reflections*. "I could not get on with it; at the end of the first page I had to send for my apothecary to ask the meaning of some allusion to his profession, which I could not understand: at the end of the second I had to send to my carpenter to explain to me," &c. &c. Elwyn quoted what he had himself heard Burke say in a speech towards the end of the Hastings' trial. "You might as well attempt to make a perfumer of a man who was bred on a dunghill, as to think of making a statesman out of this bullock contractor." In talking of America with Labouchere, it appeared from his account, that though there is no intolerance in the *laws* of that country, there is abundance of it in society; particularly among the northern states, where a man that does not go to a church of some kind forfeits caste, and in any election for a public office would not stand the slightest chance. It seems as if a certain portion of religious malice must exist in every community, and where the laws are free from it the people take it up.

June 25 Went to the Exhibition to meet Mrs Shelley; a good deal of talk about Lord B. and Shelley. Seems to have known Byron thoroughly, and always winds up her account of his bad traits with "but still he was very nice." From the Exhibition went with her to the Panorama of Geneva; pointed out to me the place where Lord B. lived. She and Shelley had a small house near him. At first they lived at Secheron, and she spoke of Byron's singing one of my Melodies, *When he who adores Thee*, as he left them in his boat of an evening, and their standing at the wall at the bottom of the garden listening to his voice over the water. Said the three of four months she passed there were the happiest of her life. The story of Lord B.'s saying to Polidori that, though Shelley did not fight, *he* did, is true.

June 27 Dined at Baring's. Company: Charles Fox and his wife, Lord Essex, Rogers, Brougham, &c. Francis Baring, whom I sat next, told me of his having met, during his travels in South America, some Mexican women who had learnt English for the express purpose of singing my Melodies. Corunna formerly called "the Groyne." Fox, in one of his speeches, calls it so. After dinner, in talking of Peter Coxe, the auctioneer,

F. Baring said, "Didn't he write some poem about 'Human Life'?" (Rogers was sitting beside him.) There was a dead silence. "No," answered Brougham at last, putting his finger up to his nose with a look of grave malice; "no it was not *Peter Coxe* that was the author of *Human Life*." B.'s look and voice irresistible, and there was a burst of laughter over the table, in which Rogers himself joined.

July 1 To Kentish Town to breakfast with Mrs Shelley. Gave me, written down, her recollections of the "Memoirs." Told me all the circumstances of poor Shelley's death. Showed me a very clever letter of Lord Byron's to her on the subject of Hunt, who had complained of some part of Lord B.'s conduct to him. She thought it a "hard and high" tone he takes with Hunt, and there may be a little too much of this in it, but it is the letter of a clever man of the world. In speaking of Hunt's claim on his friendship, he says he had always served him as far as lay in his power, but that friendship was out of the question, there being but one man (Lord Clare) for whom he entertained that feeling, "and perhaps (he adds afterwards) Thomas Moore."

September 12 A good deal of talk at breakfast about Lord Dudley; his two voices; squeak and bass; seems, as some one said, "like Lord Dudley conversing with Lord Ward"; his manner of rehearsing in an under voice what he is going to say, so that people who sit near can overhear what he is about to utter to the company. Somebody who proposed to walk a little way with him heard him mutter, in this sort of consultation with himself, "I think I may endure him for ten minutes."... The Fieldings to dinner. Talked of Porson; one of his *scherzi*, the translation of "Three blue beans in a blue bladder," τρεις κυανοι κυαμοι &c. The coolness with which he received the intelligence (which Raine trembled to communicate to him) of the destruction by fire of his long laboured *Photius*; he merely quoted "To each his sufferings, all are men," adding, "let us speak no more on the subject," and next day patiently began his work all again. At some college dinner, where, in giving toasts, the name was spoken from one end of the table, and a quotation applicable to it was to be supplied from the other, on the name of Gilbert Wakefield being given out, Porson, who hated him, roared forth, "What's Hecuba to him, or he to Hecuba?" Said one night, when he was very drunk, to Dodd, who was pressing him hard in an argument, "Jemmy Dodd, I always despised you when sober, and I'll be damned if I'll argue with you now that I'm drunk."

October 5 Set off with Dalby after breakfast to the park. Walked over the house, and felt deeply interested by it; everything looked so familiar, so redolent of old times. The breakfast-room, the old clock, and the letter boxes on each side of it, all remaining the same as they were near thirty years ago, when I felt myself so grand at being the inmate of such a great house. It seemed as if it was but yesterday I had left it, and I almost expected at every turn to see the same people meeting me with

the same looks. But, alas! what surprised me was to
find that I had all the *pictures* so thoroughly by heart,
for I certainly did not much care about painting when
I was young, and knew still less of it than I do now.
Yet there was not a figure in any of the landscapes
that did not seem to be as familiar as my own face. The
portrait of Galileo with his head leaning so thoughtfully
on his hand, and seeming to say, with a sort of mournful
resolution, *et tamen movetur*; the pretty Nell Gwynne,
the brawny Venus, professing to be a Titian, &c. &c.
Walked round the pond, that hopeless pond! in endeavouring to fill which Lord Moira expended so much
trouble and money without success; the water still
escaping like his own wealth, through some invisible
and unaccountable outlets, and leaving it dry. If anything was wanting to show the uselessness of experience
to mankind, it would be found in what I now witnessed.
From 1799 to 1812 I had seen workmen incessantly
employed in puddling and endeavouring to staunch this
unfortunate pond, and now, in 1827, I found about a
dozen or fifteen robust fellows up to their knees in the
mud, at the same wise employment. *Oh curas hominum!*
Poor Lord Hastings! I remember Rogers once saying
(as he read the inscription on the dial in the yard here),
Eheu fugaces! "He means his *estates*, I suppose."

October 17 Dined with O'Neil; a *table d'hôte*; excellent
dinner; more than twenty of the party; and almost all
Irish; among others, Mr Trevor, the son of Lord
Dungannon, and young Plunket, *the Plunket's* son.
Mr Trevor mentioned Lord — going to a fancy ball

at Florence as the hero of his own novel, and as nobody had read the novel, nobody, of course, could make out his character, so that he was obliged to inform them, "Voyez, regardez, je suis mon livre." Plunket told some things of Scott, when he was at his father's; his painful exhibition in scrambling into St Kevin's bed. Somebody said to one of the guides who attended him, "Well, how do you like that gentleman? that's Sir Walter Scott, the great poet." "A poet," answered the fellow. "No, no, the devil a poet he is, but a real gentleman, for he gave me half-a-crown."

October 19 Find that no coach leaves Cheltenham for Bath on Sunday, so resolved to excuse myself to Mr Prescott, and be off on Saturday. Got hold of Mr Millet, another of the persons I came to look after; walked with him to his house; his wife, who is dead, was intimate with Miss Chaworth, and saw a good deal of Byron when he was a boy: said that Miss C. did not like Byron, nor did his wife, nor any of the girls. Showed me a poem in Byron's handwriting, written apparently soon after he left Harrow: doubted at first whether it was really Byron's handwriting, but on further examination concluded that it was: took a copy of it, preserving all its bad spelling. A note at my hotel directed "To the immortal Thomas Moore, Esq."; only think of an immortal *esquire*; expected to hear the chambermaids cry out "Some hot water for the immortal gentleman in No. 18."

October 27 ... After luncheon walked out with Rogers; a good deal of talk about Byron; took the following memorandums, of which some are intelligible only to myself. In talking of B.'s being in love so early, R. said that Canova once told him that he (Canova) was in love at five years old. R.'s account of the old hag of a woman that was servant at Byron's lodgings in Benett Street. When he moved to the Albany, the first day I called upon him, the door was opened by the same old woman. "Why (said I to him), I thought she belonged to Benett Street, and that in getting rid of those lodgings you also got rid of the hag." "Why, yes," said Byron, "but the poor old devil took such an interest in me, that I did not like to leave her behind me." Well, in two or three years afterwards Byron was married, had a fine house in Piccadilly, two carriages, &c. &c. I called one day and (the two carriages and all the servants being out) the same old woman appeared at the door, dressed out very smart, with a new gown and a new wig. Was once going out of the Opera or some assembly with Byron, and a link boy lighted them along, saying, "This way, my Lord, this way." "Why, how does he know you are a Lord?" said Rogers. "How does he know!" answered Byron, "every one knows it; I am deformed." His great shyness of women.... The day Lord B. read the *Edinburgh Review* on his early poems, drank three bottles of claret. Some friend coming in said, "Have you received a challenge?" After writing twenty lines of the satire, got better; after a few more lines, better still.... Rogers mentioned being with Byron at the church of the Santa Croce, and though there were Machiavel, Michael Angelo, and others to engage his attention, B. continued to stand before the tomb of Galileo, saying, "I have a pleasure in looking upon that monument; he was *one of us*," meaning noble. Talked of the first day R. had him to dine to meet me. R.'s consternation when he found that he would not eat or drink any of the things that were at the table; asked for biscuits, there were none; soda water, there was none; finished by dining on potatoes and vinegar. It was upon receiving a letter from Miss Milbank (in answer to one in which he said, that though her father and mother had often asked him to their house, she never had), containing the words, "I invite you," that he sent in his second proposal for her. Used not to dine with Lady B.; had a horror of seeing women eat; his habit of offering presents; giving Rogers the picture; had given it, in the same nominal way, to two or three other people. Mentioned the letter he wrote to Murray in consigning to him the remains of little Allegra: sent the invoice, "Received two packages, contents unknown," &c. &c. Directions about the place of burial; said *first*, under the tree, and then, "on second thoughts," in the doorway of the church. The objection to the original inscription being put was that the date proclaimed it to be a child born in adultery. (Is there any inscription now?) Took it into his head before he went abroad, that he had *not* sold the copyright of his works to Murray; reference made to Rogers, when it appeared that he *had* regularly sold them to him and his heirs for ever.

Same party at dinner with the exception of Crabbe. What the Prince de Ligne said to a person, who had been trying unsuccessfully to make a piece of water in his grounds, and who told him that there had been a man drowned in it, "C'était un flatteur." In talking of dogs a case mentioned, where a man in going to bathe, left his clothes in care of his dog, but on his returning out of the water, the dog, not knowing him, would not give them up again. Dunning once being asked how he contrived to get through his business, answered, "I do a little; a little does itself; and the rest is undone." Fazakerley mentioned that he was in company with Talleyrand and Pozzo di Borgo the evening the account of Buonaparte's death arrived (I, myself, dined in company with Pozzo di Borgo that day). Talleyrand frequently said, in speaking of him, "Homme prodigieux." Pozzo and Napoleon were brought up together, but afterwards quarrelled; they belonged to the two opposite factions by which Corsica has always been agitated, and in which, it is said, the old Madame Mere took, to the last, more interest than in all the grandest affairs of Europe. Forgot to mention, as an instance of the treacherousness of the memory, that Rogers mentioned to me, among the remarkable things he remembered of Lord Byron, that it was he who came to him the evening of Percival's assassination to inform him of the event, whereas (as I soon brought to his recollection) it was *I* that called upon him that evening with the intelligence, and found him sitting with Wordsworth and Sir George Beaumont, who had dined with him.

February 2 After breakfast walked over to Kegworth to see Dr Parkinson; walked with him in his garden;

will be eighty-three his next birthday. Saw me out of the town and called upon Mrs Ingram in our way. She and her daughters accompanied me through the fields till we met the Dalby girls. Dinner at two; my company consisted of seven damsels (five of them young and pretty), Dalby being out on business. A very merry party: when I went upstairs to pack for departure, heard them in loud chorus below, and when I came down, found the seven nymphs standing, with bumpers in their hands round the table, and singing my own glee, "Hip, hip, hurrah!" to my health. Escorted by them all to the coach, in which I started at three for Nottingham.

February 7 After breakfast walked out with Bessy. Called at Murray's, and heard in a few words (while Bessy waited for me in the street) his proposition, which was to place all the publishable parts of his Byron papers in my hands, and to give me 4000 guineas for the "Life." Told him that I considered this offer perfectly liberal, but that he knew how I was situated with the Longmans, and that I certainly could not again propose to take my work out of their hands without having it in my power to pay down the sum that I owe them. "They would, I suppose (he said), be inclined to give some accommodation in the payment?" "I cannot at all answer for that, Mr Murray (I replied). I must have it in my power to offer them the payment of the debt." "Very well, sir (he said), you *may* do so." Went with Bessy to the jeweller's to buy a present for Dr Brabant's daughter: bought a locket; four guineas and a half. As Brabant will not take any fees, I must, at least, try to show that we are grateful.

February 19 Called upon Lord Sligo, and had some conversation about Lord B. Spoke of the story which Byron always said was the foundation of the *Giaour*. Sligo says, they were both riding together near Athens, when they met people bringing a girl along to be drowned; she was sitting wrapped up on a horse. Byron, by his interference, saved her. Lord Sligo did not seem very accurate in his memory of the transaction; is sure he never saw or knew anything of her before that encounter. She was afterwards sent to Thebes. One day when he was talking with Byron on the shore of the Gulf of Lepanto, Byron (who had before said that he would tell him some time why he hated his mother so much) pointed to his naked leg and foot, and said, "There's the reason; it was her false delicacy at my birth that was the cause of that deformity; and yet afterwards she reproached me with it, and not long before we parted for the last time, uttered a sort of imprecation on me, praying that I might be as ill-formed in mind as I was in body." S. said that Byron that day bathed without trowsers...... Byron's offer to Lord Sligo to go and dig for him (in the neighbourhood of Elis, I think) for antiquities. Said, "*Dilettanti*, you know, are all thieves, but you may depend upon my not stealing, because I would not give three half-pence for all the antiquities in Greece." Described Byron after his illness at Patras looking in the glass and saying, "I look pale; I should like to die of a consumption." "Why?" "Because the ladies would all say, 'Look at that poor Byron, how interesting he looks in dying.'" At Athens he used to take the bath three times a week to thin himself, and drink vinegar and water, eating only a little rice. Lord S.'s time with him at Athens was after Hobhouse left him. Went with Keppel to his lodgings, 28, Bury St. (formerly 27), for the purpose of seeing the rooms where he lives (second floor), which were my abode off and on for ten or twelve years. The sight brought back old times; it was there I wrote my *Odes and Epistles from America*, and in the parlour Strangford wrote most of his *Camoens*. In that second floor I had an illness of eight weeks, of which I was near dying, and in that shabby little second floor, when I was slowly recovering, the beautiful Duchess of St Albans (Miss Mellon) to my surprise one day paid me a visit.

February 21 Met Clark on the subject of the draft of the agreement. Went to call on Fletcher, Lord Byron's servant; some talk with him: but one can seldom get anything out of the fellow but blustering; *that* tribute to the memory of his master he is always ready with. Says he does not believe Lord Sligo, "nor any other Lord," that would say they had ever seen Byron's foot, no one ever having been allowed to see it, since the surgeons who attended him when a boy, except himself —Fletcher. Did not seem to like to talk about it, but told me, what was very striking, that even in dying Lord B. shrunk away when those about him put their

hands near his foot, as if fearing that they should un-
cover it. Said, however, that there was nothing wrong
in the shape of the foot, except being smaller than the
other, and the leg and thigh on that side a little emaciated.
Always wore trowsers (nankeen) in bathing. Latterly
led a very quiet life in Italy, but while at Venice was
as profligate as need be. Great placability in his temper,
and used always to make amends for any momentary
burst of passion by his kindness afterwards. When he
was dying told Fletcher that there was a box of 8000
dollars, of which Tita was to have 2000, and he,
Fletcher, the remainder.

February 23 Called upon Jackson, the pugilist. Showed
me two or three letters of Lord B.'s, which I copied
out. Said he had often seen B.'s foot, which had been
turned round with instruments; the limb altogether a
little wasted; could run very fast. In talking of his
courage, said that nobody could be more fearless;
showed great spirit always "in coming up to the blows."
In Jackson's visits to him to Brighton used always to
pay the chaise for him up and down. Very liberal of
his money.

May 23 Rogers having told me he was to meet Scott
this morning at breakfast with Chantrey, went there
early. Found Scott sitting to Chantrey, with Rogers,
Coke of Norfolk, and Allan Cunningham assisting.
Talked of Sir Alexander M.—(I think) and his son,
on whom the following conundrum was made: "Why
is Sir A. like a Lapland winter?" "Because he is a

long night (Knight) and his sun (son) never *shines.*"
When Sir W. went away Chantrey begged of R. and
me to stay and keep Coke in talk during his sitting to
him. Got him upon old times; told a strange story
(which I find Rogers more inclined to swallow than
I am) of a dinner given by Lord Petre to Fox and Burke
after their great quarrel, and of a contrivance prepared
by Lord Petre to introduce the subject of their difference,
and afford an opportunity of making it up. This was
no less than a piece of confectionery in the middle of the
table representing the Bastille! "Come, Burke," said
Lord Petre, at the dessert, "attack that Bastille."
Burke declined. "Well, Fox," continued his Lordship,
"Do *you* do it." "That I will, by G——," said Fox, and
instantly dashed at it. *Credat Judæus.* I doubt much
whether they *ever* met again after that quarrel. Came
away with Rogers. A letter from Bowring, informing
me that he was preparing copies for me of Lord Byron's
correspondence with him; and, strange to say, opening
up at once, without any reserve, the subject of my
attack upon him in *The Ghost of Miltiades;*" "you have
written bitter things of me," he says. He then expresses
a strong desire for a few moments' conversation with
me, adding that he thinks he could, in a few words,
remove the impression I had of his conduct. Went to
Col. Bailey's, having promised his daughter on Wednesday evening (in order to get off singing then) to come
and sing for her this morning. Found Mrs Wilson,
&c. &c. Was in good voice, and with *The Song of the
Olden Time* drew tears from the young beauties around
me. Dined at Lord Lansdowne's, and finished with

the second act of Sontag's *Donna Anna*, in the Countess St Antonio's box. Not a bad day altogether. Walter Scott, Rogers, and Chantrey, at breakfast; music and Miss Bailey at luncheon time; dinner at Lansdowne House, with the Venus of Canova before my eyes, and Sontag in the evening. Taking it with all its et ceteras of genius, beauty, feeling, and magnificence, no other country but England could furnish out such a day.

May 25 Nobody at breakfast but Lord and Lady H. and myself. Lord H. wheeled in his gouty chair, but with a face as gay and shining as that of a schoolboy, holding in his hand an epigram, which he charged me with having written and sent to his room. In speaking of the passage from one of Lord Byron's papers, in which he says that he himself and I were the only authors of the day who had an opportunity of seeing high life thoroughly, "he from birth, and I from circumstances," Lord Holland said it was not so; it was *not* from his birth that Lord Byron had taken the station he held in society, for till his talents became known, he was, in spite of his birth, in anything but good society, and *but* for his talents would never, perhaps, have been in any better. In talking of the feeling he had towards the men he lived with, Lord H. said, "*you* were the only literary person he formed an intimacy with who was 'hail fellow, well met' with him; the others he was rather inclined to insult." The anecdote about Lord H.'s expostulation with him on his attack on Lord Carlisle's paralysis; his horror at finding that Lord C. was really paralytic, and saying, (while he pointed to his foot,)

"Me, good God! *me*, of all men, to attack personal infirmities!" It was in the preface to the *Corsair* that he intended to make the explanation on this subject, but gave it up in consequence of the attack upon him in the *Courier*. Thinks Lord B. "had a twist"; his sister always told him he resembled Lord Carlisle. Asked Lord H. about the story Napier tells of Sir W. Scott having written a song for the "Pitt Club," while Fox was dying, the burden of which was "Tally-ho to the Fox." Not a word of truth in it, as I told Napier when he mentioned the wretched calumny. Scott *did*, rather unjustifiably, write a squib against the "Talents" not long after they gave him (when they might have withheld it) the place he now holds, and there *was* some fellow (Lord H. believes) who at the "Pitt Club" yelled out "Tally-ho to the Fox"; out of these two circumstances it was not difficult to trump up the story Napier tells....

Left Holland House in time to get to Rogers's, where Sir W. Scott was to call for us. Called at three to take us to dine with his son, Major Scott, at Hampton. Scott very agreeable on the way; told him our conversation at H. House about ghosts, which brought on the same topic. His own strong persuasion, one night, that he saw the figure of Lord Byron; had been either talking of or reading him, and on going into the next room was startled to see through the dusk what he could have sworn was Byron, standing as he used to do when alive. On returning into the drawing-room, he said to his daughter, "If you wish to see Lord Byron, go into that room." It was the effect of either the moonlight or twilight upon some drapery that was hanging up, which, to his imagination, just then full of Byron, presented this appearance. Rogers's story of the young couple at Berlin in their opera-box, between whom, at a distance, there always appeared to be a person sitting, though on going into their box, it was found that there was no one there but themselves. From all parts of the house this supernatural intruder could be seen; but people differed as to its appearance, some saying it was a fair man, others a dark: some maintaining that he was old, and others that he was young. It should be mentioned that there was some guilty mystery hanging over the connection between these young people; and as, at last, no one ventured to visit their box, they disappeared from Berlin. This anecdote Lord Wriothesley Russell brought with him from abroad. Scott (who evidently did not like the circumstances being left unexplained) proceeded to tell a story of Mrs Hook, the wife of Dr Hook, who wrote the "Roman History," "it being as well," he said, "to have some real person to fix one's story on." Mrs Hook becoming acquainted and intimate with a foreign lady, a widow, at Bath; their resolving to live together on their return to London. Mrs Hook, on coming down stairs one day at this lady's lodgings, meeting a foreign officer on the stairs, saying to her friend next day, "You had a visitor yesterday?" the other answering "No; she had seen no one since Mrs Hook left her." Mrs H. thinking this odd; going another day into her friend's dressing-room by mistake, and seeing the same officer there alone, stretched on the sofa. Being now sure there was something not right, determined to mention it to the lady, who, at first, said it was impossible, but on hearing a description of how the officer was dressed, fainted. Mrs Hook, convinced that it was some improper *liaison* she was carrying on, determined gradually to give up her acquaintance. The foreign lady soon after was preparing to go to London, and Mrs Hook being in the room when her maid was packing (the lady herself not being present), saw a miniature case fall out of the portmanteau, and taking it up and opening it, saw the portrait of the very person whom she had met on the stairs. "That," said the maid, "is the picture of my mistress's husband." "Her husband!" "Yes," answered the maid, "he died a short time before we left Germany." In a few weeks afterwards there arrived an order in England to have this foreign lady arrested on a charge of murdering her husband. On our arrival at Hampton (where we found the Wordsworths) walked about, the whole party, in the gay walk where the band plays, to the infinite delight of the Hampton *blues* who were all *eyes* after Scott, the other scribblers not coming in for a glance. The dinner odd, but being near Scott I found it agreeable, and was delighted to see him so happy with his tall son, the major, whom he evidently looks upon as a chevalier of romance. Told me of a tournament or joust which this son maintained once (and came off victorious) against a *Montmorency* when in barracks in— Dublin! Forgot to mention that he spoke with great delight of Mrs R. Arkwright (whom he had met at Devonshire House) and her singing. The song, *One hour with thee*, he did not at first remember to be his own words, and said to her "how pretty the words were." The Duke of Wellington, on his journey to Petersburgh, took notes all the way upon the campaign of Napoleon in Russia, having Ségur's book and some others with him.

May 27 Breakfasted at Rogers's, to meet Cooper[1] the American: Littleton and Lady Sarah, and Luttrell, also of the party. Cooper very agreeable. Anecdote of the disputatious man: "Why, it is as plain as that two and two make four." "But I deny *that* too; for two and two make twenty-two." Cooper said one thing which, more from his manner than anything else, produced a great effect; mentioning some friend of his who had been well acquainted with Lady H. Stanhope abroad, and who told him of his having, on some particular occasion, stood beside her on Mount Lebanon, when Cooper came to the word "Mount," he hesitated, and, his eyes being fixed on me, added, "I was going to say Mount Parnassus, looking at *you*." When Rogers too, in talking of Washington Irving's *Columbus*, said, in his dry significant way, "It's rather *long*," Cooper turned round on him, and said sharply, "That's a *short* criticism." Remained some time afterwards with Rogers.

May 28 Called on Lady Elizabeth Belgrave, and met there Lady Stafford and Lady Cawdor. Lady S. very gracious: the first time, I think, we have met since a memorable night at her house when the Regent was

---

[1] James Fenimore Cooper (1789-1851), the author of *The Last of the Mohicans*, etc.

there. Wishing to have a peep at him, I got in the third tier of the circle around him, and found myself placed next to Brummell. Presently the persons before us cleared away, and left him and me exposed to the Regent and his party, consisting of Lady Hertford, Duchess of R., &c. Brummell being rather comical, I could not help laughing with him a little, which I felt at the moment was unlucky, both of us being such *marked* men, though in different ways, with his R.H.; and, accordingly, I found afterwards that the Duchess of R. represented us everywhere as having stood impudently together, quizzing the Regent. Brummell himself confirmed this to me, and added, in his own way, "But she shall suffer for it; I'll chase her from society; she shall not be another fortnight in existence." All this, however, my Lady seemed to have forgot now, and was all graciousness.

June 1 Breakfasted with Rogers, the Wordsworths, and Luttrell. A quatrain quoted by Wordsworth about the Shelleys:—

> 'Twas not my wish
> To be Sir Bysshe,
> But 'twas the whim
> Of my son Tim.

All assailed me about some American lady, Miss Douglas, who, it seemed, was dying to see me, and had called once or twice at my lodgings with Sydney Smith. Agreed to send for her, and she came, carrying in her hand a little well-printed American edition of my Melodies and Sacred Songs. Told me a long story about it; that it was a clergyman made her a present of it, &c. Mentioned also a beautiful friend of hers, who had been "very gay," and a great admirer of my poetry; when she was dying she wished to hear some sacred music; and this Miss Douglas brought a person to her to sing one of my Sacred Songs, *Were not the sinful Mary's tears*, but did not think it right to tell her that the words were by the same poet she had so delighted in in her days of pleasure. Wordsworth produced an album for us all to write in, Rogers, Luttrell, and myself. Miss Douglas, by-the-bye, also told me of Miss Emmett, the daughter of him who went to America; her abstaining, at all times, from speaking of Ireland, as a subject she could not trust herself with; but one night, having been prevailed on to sing my song, *Weep on, weep on, your hour is past*, she burst into tears before she was half-way through it; and starting up from the pianoforte gave at once full vent to all her feelings about Ireland, execrating England in the most passionate manner, and wishing that America and the other nations of the earth would join to avenge Ireland's cause on her.

June 4 Breakfasted with Harness; Newton and I went together; the rain desperate. Harness mentioned that he saw once a collection of all the reviews that had appeared upon Byron's early poems, noted in the margin by his mother, Mrs Byron (who had got them all bound together), and the remarks not such as gave Harness the idea of a very ignorant or incapable woman. Some discussion with respect to Byron's *chanting* method of repeating poetry, which I professed my strong dislike of. Observe, in general, that it is the men who have the worst ears for music that *sing* out poetry in this manner, having no nice perception of the difference there ought to be between animated reading and *chant*. This very much the Harrow style of reading. Hodgson has it; Lord Holland, too (though not I believe, a Harrow man), gives in to it considerably. Harness himself, I perceived, had it strongly; and, by his own avowal, he is without a musical ear, as is Lord Holland to a remarkable degree. Lord Byron, though he loved simple music, had no great organisation that way.

June 6 Set off for town in the coach at nine. Dined at Rogers's. Company: Lord Clifden, Lord and Lady Gage, the Lubbocks, C. Fox, Lady Devy, Jekyll, &c. &c. Sat next to Jekyll, and was, as usual, amused. In talking of figurative oratory, mentioned the barrister before Lord Ellenborough. "My Lord, I appear before you in the character of an advocate from the city of London; my Lord, the city of London herself appears before you as a suppliant for justice. My Lord, it is written in the book of nature—" "What book?" says Lord E. "The book of nature." "Name the page," says Lord E., holding his pen uplifted, as if to note the page down. An addition to our party in the evening, among whom was Mrs Siddons; had a good deal of conversation with her, and was, for the first time in my life, interested by her off the stage. She talked of the loss of friends, and mentioned herself as having lost twenty-six friends in the course of the last six years. It is something to have *had* so many. Among other reasons for her regret at leaving the stage was, that she always found in it a vent for her private sorrows, which enabled her to bear them better; and often she has got credit for the truth and feeling of her acting when she was doing nothing more than relieving her own heart of its grief. This, I have no doubt, is true, and there is something particularly touching in it. Rogers has told me that she often complained to him of the great *ennui* she has felt since she quitted her profession, particularly of an evening. When sitting drearily alone, she has remembered what a moment of excitement it used to be when she was in all the preparation of her toilette to meet a crowded house and exercise all the sovereignty of her talents over them. *Apropos* of loss of friends, somebody was saying the other day, before Morgan, the great calculator of lives, that they had lost so many friends (mentioning the number) in a certain space of time, upon which Morgan, coolly taking down a book from his office shelf, and looking into it, said, "So you ought, Sir, and *three more*."

June 10 Called with fear and trembling at Benett's for my letter from Bess; found it far more comfortable than I expected; the leeches have removed the spasms. Went to Longmans, and Rees accompanied me to the Royal Exchange to call upon a person connected with Cefalonia (Mr Hancock), on the subject of Lord Byron. Rees mentioned Sir W. Scott having said of me that I was (in manners and habits) a truly *gentleman* poet. In something of the same feeling, Scott said of

Wordsworth (as we were going down to Hampton), that he was in society, *too much of the poet.*

January 3 Walked over to Bowood to dinner. The only addition to the company a Russian, whose name nobody could pronounce for me. A very intelligent man, and much versed in the literature of England, as well as of every other part of Europe. Told me that there were two translations of my *Irish Melodies* into Russian, and that he had with him the translation of my *Peri*, made by the Russian poet who accompanied the present Empress when she was at Berlin. In the evening sang a good deal. The Russian showed me the translation of my *Peri* in a collection of Russian poems which he had bound together to read in travelling. My name in the Russian was made *Murosou*, the *ou* at the end being, as in Greek, the sign of the genitive case, "of Moore." Walter Scott not at all to be recognised in its Russian shape.

February 9 to 12 A melancholy week, but lucky for me that I am *obliged* to work, as it, in some degree, distracts my thoughts. The dreadful moment is that interval at night, when I have done working and am preparing for bed. It is then everything most dreadful crowds upon me, and the loss not only of this dear child, but of all that I love in the world, seems impending over me. Nothing could surpass the kindness of the Fieldings and everybody else. A letter from Lady Lansdowne offering Bessy and me rooms at Bowood whenever we might wish to go there. Our poor girl sometimes cheerful, and the night before last not only made me play some waltzes to her, but hummed one or two herself.

February 22 Off at seven. Arrived at Calne before five, and set off on foot for home. Felt most anxious as I approached the cottage, not knowing what might have happened since the day before yesterday. Could not bring myself to enter at the hall-door, but tapped at the back kitchen window in order to know what I was to expect. Our poor child much the same; found her upstairs in the room she was never again to leave *alive*.

February 23 *to* 28 The next fortnight furnishes but a melancholy detail of the last hours of our darling child, the only consolation of which was that she passed them without suffering, and even in calm and cheerful enjoyment. She had no idea of her danger, nor did Bessy, nor I, nor any of those about her, ever show the least sign of alarm or sorrow in her presence. There are some pious persons who would think this wrong, and who would have disturbed and embittered the last moments of this innocent child with religious exhortations and *preparations* (as they would call it) for another world, as if the whole of her short and stainless life was not a far better preparation than any that their officiousness could afford her. We passed every evening together (she, and I, and her mamma) in some amusement or other, and as it had been seldom in my power to spare so much of my company in this way, it was a treat to her which she enjoyed most thoroughly. "What nice evenings we have!" she would say to her mamma continually. Sometimes we used to look over together a child's book in which there were pictures from history, and talk of the events and persons they alluded to; at another time, Caroline Fielding's sketch-book and the engravings of Pinelli were an amusement to her; but, in general, what gave her pleasure was either playing a game or two at draughts with me herself, or looking on while her mamma and I played draughts or cribbage, and betting with me as to which should win. However difficult it was to go on cheerfully in such circumstances, I am convinced that the effort did both Bessy and me much service, by accustoming us to control our feelings, and, in a certain degree, *hardening* us for the worst. I have already mentioned her having attempted to sing through a quadrille one evening, a little before my departure for town, and at the same time she gave an imitation of a foreigner whom she had heard counterfeiting the tones of different musical instruments with his voice at Devizes. A few nights after my return (on the 27th I think) she said to her mamma, when she was putting her to bed (having been all the evening in most cheerful spirits), "Shall I try and sing?" "Do, love," said her mamma, and she immediately sung the line, "When in death I shall calm recline," without, however, (as Bessy is persuaded) having the least idea of applying it to her own situation.

March 1 *to* 12 Towards the end of this week she began to have *accesses* of extra weakness in the mornings, so much so as to make me think, each time, that her last moment was come; but she revived from them after taking some refreshment, and the strong cheerful tone of her voice on recovering from what had appeared to be death seemed wonderful, and even startling. Sunday, 8th, I rose early, and on approaching the room, heard the dear child's voice as strong, I thought, as usual; but, on entering, I saw death plainly in her face. When I asked her how she had slept, she said, "Pretty well," in her usual courteous manner; but her voice had a sort of hollow and distant softness not to be described. When I took her hand on leaving her, she said (I thought significantly), "Good bye, papa." I will not attempt to tell what I felt at all this. I went occasionally to listen at the door of the room, but did not go in, as Bessy, knowing what an effect (through my whole future life) such a scene would have upon me, implored me not to be present at it. Thus passed the first of the morning. About eleven o'clock (as Bessy told me afterwards) the poor child, with an appearance rather of wandering in her mind, said, somewhat wildly, "I shall die, I shall die"; to which her mamma answered, "We pray to God continually for you, my dear Anastasia, and I am sure God must love you, for you have been always a good girl." "Have I?" she said; "I thought I was a very naughty girl; but I am glad to hear *you* say that I have been good; for others would perhaps say it out of compliment, but you know me, and must therefore think so, or you would not say it." "But everybody thinks the same, my love. All your young friends love you. Lady Lansdowne thinks you a very good girl." "Does she, mummy?" said the dear child; and then added, "Do you think I shall go to Lady Lansdowne's party this year?" I don't know what poor Bessy answered to this. In about three-quarters of an hour or less she called for me, and I came and took her hand for a few seconds, during which Bessy leaned down her head between the poor dying child and me, that I might not see her countenance. As I left the room, too, agonised as her own mind was, my sweet, thoughtful Bessy ran anxiously after me, and giving me a smelling-bottle, exclaimed, "For God's sake don't *you* get ill." In about a quarter of an hour afterwards she came to me, and I saw that all was over. I could no longer restrain myself; the feelings I had been so long suppressing found vent, and a fit of loud violent sobbing seized me, in which I felt as if my chest was coming asunder. The last words of my dear child were "Papa, papa." Her mother had said, "My dear, I think I could place you more comfortably, shall I?" to which she answered, "Yes," and Bessy placing her hand under her back, gently raised her. That moment was her last. She exclaimed suddenly, "I am dying, I am dying, Papa! papa!" and expired.

On the 12th our darling child was conveyed to Bromham churchyard, poor Bessy having gone the night before to see where she was to be laid. Almost all those offices towards the dead which are usually left to others to perform, the mother on this occasion would perform herself, and the last thing she did before the coffin was closed on Wednesday night, was to pull some snowdrops herself and place them within it. She had already, indeed, laid on her dead darling's bosom a bunch of cowslips, which she had smelled to (and with *such* eagerness) the day before her death, and it was singular enough, and seemed to give Bessy pleasure, that though lying there three days they were scarcely at all faded. I had ordered a chaise on the morning of the funeral to take us out of the way of this most dreadful ceremony, (well remembering how it harrowed up all our feelings in following my poor father to the grave,) and a most melancholy drive we had of it for two long hours, each bearing up for the sake of the other, but all the worse, in reality, for the effort.

And such is the end of so many years of fondness and hope; and nothing is now left us but the dream (which may God in his mercy realise) that we shall see our pure child again in a world more worthy of her.

May 7 Stayed at home in the morning, correcting. Dined at Lord Lansdowne's: the Cowpers, the Hopes, Lord W. Russell, Lord Villiers, Caroline Fielding, the George Lambs, &c. A good deal of conversation with Lord W. Russell in the evening about Byron; his dissipation at Venice; doing it very much out of bravado, and not really liking it. Used often to fly away from home and row all night upon the water. Mentioned what he had heard of Byron's not feeling any admiration of Rome; saying to Hobhouse, "What shall I write about?" and H. giving him the heads of what he afterwards described so powerfully.

May 23 Breakfasted at the Athenæum for the purpose of meeting Mr Matthews, with whom I had been lately corresponding so much about his brother, &c. &c. The parody on *Eloisa to Abelard*, so generally attributed to Porson, was, it seems, really written by Mr Matthews's father. Had rather a painful scene this morning. While I was knocking at Lord Ilchester's door, Lord Anglesey, with his daughters, drove up to his own; and calling me over, seized me by the arm, and said, "Now that I have caught you, I will not let you go till you hear my daughter sing, and sing something in return for her." In vain did I protest that I was in a hurry somewhere upon business; he would hear of nothing, but forced me upstairs, where I was introduced, for the first time, to his lady. The girl was set down instantly in a bustle to the pianoforte, and sung my *Common Sense and Genius*, which Lord A. declared to be his especial favourite. I was then obliged (in spite of various protestations about want of voice, long time since I sung, &c. &c.) to take my seat at the pianoforte; and the moment I sat down, felt that I should make a fool of myself. With difficulty I got through *When he who adores thee*; but when I came to *Keep your tears for me*, the melancholy sound of my own voice quite overpowered me; and had I not started up instantly, I should have burst into one of my violent sobbing fits, which, before strangers, would have been dreadful. I never was better pleased than to find myself in the street once more. When shall I be able to sing again? The thought of my dear child comes across me at these moments with a gush of bitterness which is indescribable.

May 30 ... Called upon Miss Crump, and found Lord Dillon with her. His description of the way in which he lives at Ditchley; reading aloud of an evening all "the good old coarse novels," *Peregrine Pickle* particularly, because Commodore Trunnion was his (Lord Dillon's) uncle. Told of the manner in which this uncle died. His old rough tar of a servant came to his room to say the carriage was ready, and then looking at his master exclaimed, "Why, you're dead on one side." "I *am*, Tim," he answered; "turn me on the other," which Tim did; and he died.

June 3 Breakfasted with Rogers: company, Sharp, Lord Lansdowne, and Hallam. R. very amusing; his account of a club to which Sharp and he belonged, called "Keep the Line." Their motto, written up in large characters, the composition of Reynolds—

> Here we eat and drink and dine—
> Equinoctial—keep the line.

Most of them being dramatists, the effect of a joke upon them, instead of producing laughter, was to make them immediately look grave (this being their business), and the tablets were out in an instant.

June 7 At home till latish. Dined at Holland House. Company: Mr Grenville, the Vernon Smiths, Mackintosh, Lord St Asaph, &c. Lord H.'s story of the man in Spain with a basket of vipers proclaiming their freshness and liveliness to a large party of travellers who slept in the same room with him. At night somebody awaked by feeling something cold passing over his face; and at the same moment the viper-merchant exclaiming aloud in the dark, "My vipers have got loose, but lie still, all of you; they will not hurt you, if you don't move," &c. &c. In the evening Lord H. showed me, according to promise, Byron's poem of the *Devil's Drive* (which he had, I must say, made a good deal of fuss about showing, nor should I have seen it at all but for my lady). A good deal disappointed by it. Lady H. asked me to come some morning, and mark what I wished extracted from it. Came away with Mr Grenville; made me the offer of his library, to make use of whatever it contained relative to Ireland. In speaking of Mackintosh, remarked (as characteristic of that distrust of himself which prevents his great acquirements from telling in society as they ought) his habit of advancing three or four steps forward while he is conversing, and then, as if suddenly recollecting himself, retiring again.

June 8 Breakfasted at the Athenæum. Two letters from my sweet Bessy within these few days, of which I cannot help transcribing some passages. I had told her in one of mine how much deeper every day the memory of our sad loss sunk into my heart. "How exactly (she says) your feeling about our sweet girl resembles mine. All last night I was with her, and had hopes of her recovery; but the light of the morning again told the same sad truth, that she was gone, and, in this world, we should never meet, but in dreams." In another part of the same letter she says: "There are three sisters here (Cheltenham), that always remind me of what our dear girls might have been. It is not that they are at all like any of our dears, but they are three in number, and about a year or so between them, dressed alike, and full of the life and happiness so beautiful at that age. There are, indeed, many other children here, that often make me sigh; and there are times when the sweet music and their happy faces and firm step make me feel most sad and lonely in the midst of all the gaiety; but I do not indulge more than is quite necessary to me, and I trust I shall meet you, improved and strengthened, both in mind and body." In the second letter, announcing her coming, she says: "I am already, thank God, better; but it is my mind that prevents me from going on as well as you could wish. Every day only adds to the loneliness of the future, and the happy face of that sweet child is for ever before me, as she used to sit at the other side of the table. But I will try and only think of her as I trust she *is*,—happy, and often looking down on those she so tenderly loved. How she thought of and loved *you*! Her dear eyes were always full of light if you but went upstairs, and she thought there was a chance of your coming into the parlour. Though my thoughts are melancholy, and my heart sad, still I have great, very great blessings; and if God but allows me to live for and with the three beings that are still left, I must be happy." Bless her admirable heart! At a quarter past four was at the coach-office to receive little Tom from Southampton; deposited him at Power's; and, between seven and eight, went to receive Bessy also, who came last from Buckhill.

June 11 Dined at Power's, and off again to the Charter House in the evening, to deliver up our young Carthusian into the hands of the old matron. Sent for Sydney Smith's son, the only boy whose father I thought I knew, to introduce Tom to him. Brought with him a son of Sir James Montgomery, who is also on the foundation, while the matron sent for the boy that was to be Tom's monitor. After talking to them a little, gave Smith a sovereign and a half to divide between the three. While I was doing this, Bessy took Tom aside (on whom we have always impressed the propriety of not taking money from any one but ourselves) and endeavoured to explain away the inconsistency of my doing with these boys what I did not choose should be done with him; telling him that some people did not mind their sons taking money, but that he knew *our* feeling on the subject was quite different.

August 12 Breakfasted with Mrs Shelley. In talking of Byron's religion, mentioned a book, *Easy Way with Deists*, which made a great impression upon him. Shelley undertook to answer it; but when he had got through six pages, stopped in his task, saying that Byron was a person who wanted checks rather than otherwise. Byron shocked afterwards at the life he had led at Venice, and hated to think of it. Found out Mrs Kean, to whom I wished to put some queries. Told me about the presents from Lord B. of a box and a sword. The former has on it a representation of a boar-hunt, and was presented by him to Kean after seeing him in *Richard III*. Byron offended at Kean's leaving a dinner, which had been chiefly made for him, at which were B. himself, Lord Kinnaird, and Douglas Kinnaird. Kean pretended illness and went away early; but Byron found out afterwards that he had gone to take the chair at a pugilistic supper. B., after this, would not speak to Kean. He was, however, so delighted with his acting in Sir Giles Overreach, that, notwithstanding all this, he presented to him, immediately after seeing him in this character, a very handsome Turkish sword, with a Damascus blade. Sent him £50. at his benefit.

November 19 Pearce's account of Lord Stowell and Capt. Morris; the former saying to the latter (both being of the same age, eighty-five), "What is it that keeps you so young, Morris?" "It is all owing (says M.) to my having fallen violently in love at sixteen, and that has kept my heart warm and fresh ever since. I have married in the interim, but never forgot the impression of that first love, though the girl never knew I felt it for her." Lord Stowell pleaded guilty to the same sort of youthful passion, and it turned out, on comparing notes, that it was for the very same girl, who was a celebrated beauty in their young days in the town of Carlisle where they both lived. On coming to inquire what had become of this common object of their admiration (whom Morris supposed to have been long dead), it appeared that she too was still alive, and also in her eighty-fifth year, having changed her name from "Molly Dacre," under which they first knew her, and being now a widow. This discovery inspired old Morris's muse with some very good stanzas, of which the following are the prettiest:

>Though years have spread around my head
>   The sober veil of Reason,
>To close in night sweet Fancy's light
>   My heart rejects as treason.
>A spark there lies, still fann'd by sighs,
>   Ordained by beauty's Maker;
>And, fixed by Fate, burns yet, though late,
>   For lovely Molly Dacre.
>
>Oh, while I miss the days of bliss,
>   I passed enraptur'd gazing,
>The dream impress'd still charms my breast,
>   Which Fancy's ever raising.
>Though much I meet in life is sweet,
>   My soul can ne'er forsake her;
>And all I feel still bears the seal
>   Of lovely Molly Dacre.
>   .   .   .   .   .
>I've often thought the happy lot
>   Of health and spirits left me
>Is deem'd as due to faith so true,
>   And thus by Fate is sent me.
>While here she be [or "lives she"] there's life for me;
>   But when High Heaven shall take her,
>A like last breath I'll ask of death,
>   To follow Molly Dacre.

Lady Clarke, upon being informed of her two old lovers (for, I believe, the first time), wrote a letter to one or both, very playfully and cleverly expressed.

June 26 Tempted out from my work by the fine day and the death of his Majesty, both of which events have set the whole town in motion. Never saw London so excited or so lively. Crowds everywhere, particularly in St James's Street, from the proclamation of the new King being expected before the Palace. The whole thing reminded me of a passage in an old comedy: "What makes him so merry?" "Don't you see he's in mourning?" Dined at the Lansdownes. Company: Duke of Grafton, the Jerseys, the Morleys, the Vernons, the Lord Chancellor, &c. Sat next the Lord Chancellor, and was being amused by his manner. Was laughing at the state of nervousness Scarlett had got into on the subject of the press. Vernon told me that the first account he had of the King's death in the morning was from Botham (at Salt Hill, where Vernon and Lady Elizabeth slept), Botham saying to him, when he came downstairs, "Well, sir, I have lost my *neighbour*."

September 6 [IN IRELAND] Drove into Kilkenny, with Bryan and Bessy. In looking along the walk by the river, under the Castle, my sweet Bess and I recollected the time when we used, in our love-making days, to stroll for hours there together. We did not love half so *really* then as we do now.

September 14 [IN DUBLIN] Dined (I alone) at Crampton's. Called for by Bessy and Ellen in the evening to go to a party at Mrs Smith's. Music; sung. Have observed (what I should not have believed had I not witnessed it) that the Irish are much colder as auditors (to *my* singing, at least) than the English. Nothing like the same *empressement*, the crowding towards the pianoforte, the eagerness for more which I am accustomed to in most English companies. This may be, perhaps, from my being made so much of a *lion* here, or from some notion of good breeding and finery, some idea probably that it is more fashionable and *English* not to be too moved. From whatever reason it may proceed, it is the last thing I should have expected.

September 15 [IN DUBLIN] Day of the meeting to celebrate the late French Revolution. Went at one o'clock; Bessy, Ellen, Mrs Meara, &c., having gone before. Saw that they were well placed, and my little Tom with them. The Committee still in deliberation on the forms of proceeding. At this time more than 2000 persons collected: the room (the National Mart) being nearly full. Sheil one of the earliest speakers; his manner, action, &c., all made me tremble a little for his chances of success in the House of Commons, about which I had before felt very sanguine. His voice has no *medium* tone, and, when exerted, becomes a scream; his action theatrical, and of the *barn* order of theatricals; but still his oratorical powers great, and capable of producing (in an Irish audience at least) great excitement. It was wished that I should second the resolution he proposed, and a call to that effect was becoming very general, but I resolved not. About this time the doors, which had been closed, were burst open by the people without, and the room was completely filled: supposed to be about 3000 persons in all. After a resolution proposed by Mr Hamilton, late candidate for the county of Dublin, the call for me became obstreperous, and I rose. My reception almost astoundingly enthusiastic. For some minutes I got on with perfect self-possession, but my very success alarmed me, and I at once lost the thread of what I was about to say; all seemed to have vanished from my mind. It was a most painful moment, and Sheil (who was directly under me) told me afterwards that I had turned quite pale. I was enough collected, however, to go on saying *something*, though *what* I hardly knew, till at length my mind worked itself clear, and I again got full possession of my subject. So luckily, too, had I managed these few minutes of aberration, that, as I found afterwards, the greater part of my audience gave me credit for having assumed this momentary fit of embarrassment. From this on to the end my display was most successful; and the consciousness that every word *told* on my auditory, reacted back again on me with a degree of excitement that made me feel capable of *anything*. The shouts, the applauses, the waving of hats, &c., after I had finished, lasted for some minutes. I heard Sheil, too, as I concluded, say with some warmth, "He is a most beautiful speaker!" Found Bessy and Ellen where they sat as soon as I could, and had to make up my face to stand, for the rest of the day, the uninterrupted stare of some dozens of girls near us, many of them as good specimens of the *beau sang* of Ireland as could be found. I found that a very melancholy thought had crossed my dear Bessy's mind at the time when I paused in my speech. "He is thinking," she said to herself, "of Anastasia": and her heart beat so violently with the idea, that she thought she should have fainted. It is true I had often during the day thought with sad regret of our sweet child, and the delight she would have felt in witnessing my success had she been spared to us; but, of course, at the moment of my bewilderment I thought of nothing but how to find my way back again. It was, however, a natural consequence of the state of excitement into which Bessy had been thrown by the whole scene (for at the first peal of acclamation on my entering the room, she burst into tears) to have such sad thoughts mingle with her pleasure and triumph. The *surgit amari aliquid* is so desolatingly true! Two of the speakers that succeeded me very good, Murphy and Sheehan (editor of the *Mail*); the only two I heard that struck me as likely to do in the House of Commons. Between four and five, with some difficulty, got Bessy and Tom away (my sister having gone before). As soon as the meeting perceived me going, the acclamations were renewed; found outside a large concourse of people to receive us, who hurrahed, shook hands, &c.; and, when we got into the carriage, insisted upon taking the horses off, and drawing us home. When we had proceeded half up the quay, however, I prevailed upon them to put the horses to again, and having provided myself with a pound's worth of silver, scattered it for a scramble among my escorters, and got quietly home.

April 24 [IN LONDON] Called upon Lady Cork in the morning, who snubbed me for using the word "nice," and said that Dr Johnson would never let *her* use it.

April 28 Dined with Rogers. Company: only Sharpe, Miss Rogers, and Mrs Lockhart. Mrs L. gave a better account of Sir Walter, who has had a bad attack lately. Lockhart told me, a day or two since, that it was not apoplexy, but an affection of the stomach, which produced effects very much the same in appearance, by sending up blood to the head. Mackintosh, he said, had suffered from a similar complaint. Mrs Lockhart said, that worry and alarm at this new measure of reform had a great deal to do with it, and that just before this late attack some person had written him a letter from London containing an account of the dissolution, and the scenes in the two Houses in consequence, which threw him into a state of great nervousness and agitation. A curious conversation after dinner from my saying that, "after all, it was in high life one met the best society"; Rogers violently opposing me; he, too, of all men, who (as I took care to tell him) had through the greater part of his life shown practically that he agreed with me, by confining himself almost exclusively to this class of society. It is, indeed, the power which these great people have of commanding, among their other luxuries, the presence of such men as he is at their tables, that sets their circle (taking all its advantages into account) indisputably above all others in the way of *society*. —— said, with some bitterness, that, on the contrary, the high class were the vulgarest people one met. Vulgar enough, God knows! some of them are; vulgar in *mind*, which is the worst sort of vulgarity. But, to say nothing of women, *where*, in any rank or station in life, could one find *men* better worth living with, whether for manners, information, or any other of the qualities that render society agreeable, than such persons as Lords Holland, Grey, Carlisle, Lansdowne, Cowper, King, Melbourne, Carnarvon, John Russell, Dudley, Normanby, Morpeth, Mahon, and numbers of others that I can speak of from personal knowledge?

June 25 ...Dined at the Speaker's; none but the family, besides Corry and myself. The Speaker very agreeable: described his dinner lately with the King, on the day when all the Judges dined with him. The King had asked him that very morning at the levee, saying, "I don't well know what name to call you by, for you know you are not Speaker now; but still I will say, Mr Speaker, I am most happy to see you here, and if you have nothing better to do to-day, I wish you would come and meet the Judges at dinner." Described the manner in which the King wakes suddenly from his occasional dozes after dinner, and dashes at once into conversation. On that day he rather awkwardly, in one of these *sorties*, began upon the subject of the Queen's trial, saying that he had high respect for judges, but by no means the same feeling for lawyers, who were often led, by their zeal for their clients, to do things by no means justifiable; "As you may recollect," he added, turning to Brougham and Denman, "in a case where you, gentlemen, were concerned," &c. &c. He got out of this scrape, however (the Speaker said), very good-humouredly and skilfully. The Speaker told us several interesting anecdotes of the old King during his last melancholy years of madness, blindness, and, at last, utter deafness, which he had himself heard from his father, the Archbishop, who was one of the persons chiefly entrusted with the task of visiting and superintending the care of the Royal patient. The old King's horror at the first suggestion of a strait waistcoat, and his saying that he would go on his knees to the Archbishop if he would save him from it. His notions of kingly power to the last, and the cunning with which he contrived to keep up the appearance of it, ordering carriages and horses to be ready at a particular hour, and then taking care to *countermand* them a little before the time arrived. The Prince, not having seen him for a long time (it being found that intercourse with any of his own family excited and irritated him), was at length permitted one day to come into the apartment for a few minutes, and look at his father as he sat in his chair, without speaking. Shortly after his departure, the old King, in taking his usual exercise of walking round the room, stopped suddenly on the spot where the Prince had been standing, and said, "If I did not know it was impossible, I should say that the Prince of Wales was now in the room"; giving, as his reason, the strong smell of perfume which he perceived.

June 26 Went (Lord John and I together, in a hackney-coach) to breakfast with Rogers. The party, besides ourselves, Macaulay[1], Luttrell and Campbell. Macaulay gave us an account of the state of the *Monothelite* controversy, as revived at present among some of the fanatics of the day. In the course of conversation, Campbell quoted a line, "Ye diners out, from whom

[1] Thomas Babington Macaulay, afterwards Lord Macaulay (1800–1859), the famous historian.

we guard our spoons," and looking over at me, said
significantly, "*You* ought to know that line." I pleaded
not guilty; upon which he said, "It is a poem that
appeared in *The Times*, which every one attributed to
you"; but I again declared that I did not even remember
it. Macaulay then broke silence, and said, to our general
surprise, "That is *mine*"; on which we all expressed a
wish to have it recalled to our memories, and he repeated the whole of it. I then remembered having been
much struck with it at the time, and said that there was
another squib still better, on the subject of William
Bankes's candidateship for Cambridge, which so amused
me when it appeared, and showed such power in that
style of composition, that I wrote up to Barnes about
it, and advised him by all means to secure that hand as
an ally. "That was mine also," said Macaulay; thus
discovering to us a new power, in addition to that varied
store of talent which we had already known him to
possess. He is certainly one of the most remarkable
men of the day.

July 28 Dined at Bowles's. Party: Mulvany, a young
Irish artist, and ourselves, old Hoyle (the *Exodiad* poet),
and another person. Mentioned a pun of Pitt's, viz.
Latin for a *rimy* morning, *Aurora Musis amica*. Never
saw Bowles in more amusing plight; played for us on
the fiddle after dinner a country dance, which forty
years ago he heard on entering a ball-room, to which
he had rode, I don't know how many miles, to meet a
girl he was very fond of, and found her dancing to this
tune when he entered the room. The *sentiment* with

which he played this old-fashioned jig beyond anything diverting. I proposed we should dance to it; and taking out Mrs Bowles, led off, followed by the Powers, Bessy, Mulvany, &c. &c. Our fiddler soon tired, on which Hoyle volunteered a scrape, and played so dolefully slow, as to make us laugh in far quicker time than we danced. However, we briskened up his old bow; and Mrs Moore taking Bowles for a partner, we got through one of the most laughing dances I have seen for a long time.

Combe-Florey, Taunton.
August 11th, 1831.

My dear Moore,
From hence till the 1st September (when men of large fortune put men of no fortune in prison on account of partridges), I shall be absent. I shall be at Sidmouth till the 12th, and then a week at Lord Morley's, returning to Sidmouth for the rest of the month. I shall be at home all October. At Sidmouth we are no farther from the sea than the focus of Rogers's voice. Nothing intervenes between us and the coast of France. The noise of persons chattering French on the opposite coast is heard. Flat fish and mackerel have been known to leap into the drawing-room; and in the dreadful storm of 1824 the four Miss Somebodies were taken out in the lifeboat without petticoats by men who, in the hurry of the occasion, were without small clothes. Come to Sidmouth, and make Rogers come, and come to C.-Florey too and make Rogers come.

Ever yours,
S. Smith.

October 14 ...To dinner at Sir Walter Scott's (or rather Lockhart's). On my way to dinner, with Murray, who took me, told him that I had made up my mind to be editor at all events, and that he might announce me as such; which seemed very much to please him. Was rather shocked at seeing and hearing Scott; both his looks and utterance, but particularly the latter, showing strongly the effects of paralysis. At dinner we had, besides Murray and myself, their own family party (the Lockharts and Miss Scott), and Sir William and Lady Rae. Scott took but rarely any share in the conversation, and it was then with difficulty I made out what he said. On going up stairs found rather a large party collected, all Scotch—Lady Belhaven, Lord and Lady Ruthven, Lady Louisa Stuart, the Macleods, &c. &c. On looking over at Scott once or twice, was painfully struck by the utter vacancy of his look. How dreadful if he should live to survive that mighty mind of his! It seems hardly right to assemble company round him in this state. It is charming to see how Scott's good temper and good nature continue unchanged through the sad wreck of almost everything else that belonged to him. The great object in sending him abroad is to disengage his mind from the strong wish to *write* by which he is haunted; eternally making efforts to produce something without being able to bring his mind collectively to bear upon it—the *multum cupit, nihil potest*. Alas! alas!

October 15 Breakfasted at the Athenæum. Then on the Charter House for Tom. I then set off with him

to Sir Walter Scott's, being determined that the little
dog should have to say in future days that he had seen
this great man. Found Lord Clarendon calling at the
same time, and admitted with us: Scott very kind to
Tom. Had taken with me a book of his (the
Demonology) that he might write his name in it for
Bessy. He said that I ought to have let him have the
pleasure of giving the book as well as the name.

October 17 Breakfasted with Rogers to meet my old
friends Lord and Lady Dunmore, whom I had not met
for, I believe, ten years. Stuart also of the party, and
(by accident) Campbell, who had happened to call upon
Rogers on business: the conversation at breakfast
amusing. Campbell mentioned how his vanity was
once mortified on giving his address to some Scotch
bookseller: "Campbell!" said the man; "pray, Sir, may
you be the great Campbell?" "Who do you call the
great Campbell?" said Tom, putting on a modest look.
"Why, John Campbell, the African Traveller, to be
sure," answered the other. In talking of getting into
awkward scrapes at dinner tables, Lady Dunmore mentioned a circumstance of the kind in which Rogers
himself was concerned. It was at the time when Madame
de Staël was expected in London, and somebody at
table (there being a large party) asked when she was
likely to arrive. "Not till Miss Edgeworth is gone,"
replied Rogers; "Madame de Staël would not like *two*
stars shining at the same time." The words were hardly
out of his mouth when he saw a gentleman rise at the
other end of the table, and say in a solemn tone,

"Madame la Baronne de Staël est incapable d'une telle bassesse." It was Auguste de Staël, her son, whom Rogers had never before seen.

Left Rogers with Campbell, who told me, as we walked along, the friendly service which Rogers had just done him by consenting to advance £500., which Campbell wants at this moment to purchase a share in the new (*Metropolitan*) magazine of which he is editor, the opportunity, if let slip now, being wholly lost to him. Campbell had offered as security an estate worth between four and five thousand pounds which he has in Scotland, but Rogers had very generously said that he did not want security; Campbell, however, was resolved to give it. These are noble things of Rogers, and he does more of such things than the world has any notion of.

November 3 to 9 Saw my *Lord Edward* announced as one of the articles in the *Quarterly*, to be abused of course: and this so immediately after my dinings and junkettings with both editor and publisher! Having occasion to write to Murray, sent him the following squib:

THOUGHTS ON EDITORS

Editur et edit

No, editors don't care a button
 What false and faithless things they do;
They'll let you come and cut their mutton,
 And then they'll have a cut at you.

With Barnes I oft my dinner took,
  Nay, met ev'n Horace Twiss to please him;
Yet Mister Barnes traduced my book,
  For which may his own devils seize him!

With Doctor Bowring I drank tea,
  Nor of his cakes consumed a particle;
And yet th' ungrateful LL.D.
  Let fly at me next week an article.

John Wilson gave me suppers hot,
  With bards of fame like Hogg and Packwood,
A dose of black strap then I got,
  And after a still worse of *Blackwood*.

Alas, and must I close the list
  With thee, my Lockhart, of the *Quarterly*,
So kind, with bumper in thy fist,—
  With pen, so *very* gruff and tartarly.

Now in thy parlour feasting me,
  Now scribbling at me from thy garrett,—
Till 'twixt the two in doubt I be
  Which sourest is, thy wit or claret.

November 10 To dinner at Lacock; none beside themselves but Lord Valletort and Mademoiselle Emmeline. Had known very little of him before, and once rather disliked him; but he appears to me an honest, kindhearted man, and, though a strong Tory, seems a fair one. Told some interesting things of the Duke of Wellington, to whom he is (like all who have been much about him) strongly attached. His saying, that no man should hesitate to apologise whenever he had said or done anything that required one; yet in military affairs he has been known on more than one occasion to avoid owning he was wrong, though conscious that he *was* so. This done on principle. "No, no; never put myself wrong with the army." His shedding tears when he took leave officially of the Queen at his last resignation; this the Queen herself told Lord Valletort. Of the King, Lord V. told several little things which show great good-nature and warm-heartedness. His father and mother were (as I told him) amongst my earliest acquaintance in London. I remember how proud I used to be of going to Lady Mount Edgecumbe's suppers (one or two at the most) after the Opera. It was at one of these, sitting between Mrs Siddons and Lady Castlereagh, I heard for the first time the voice of the former, (never having met her before) transferred to the ordinary things of this world,—and the solemn words in her most tragic tone,—"I do love ale dearly."

March 27 Breakfasted at R.'s; found there Barry Cornwall and Charles Murray. Proctor's stories of Charles Lamb. His excluding from his library the works of Robertson, Hume, Gibbon, &c., and substituting for them the heroes of the *Dunciad*, of whose writings he has made a collection. His saying to ——, in his odd, stammering way, on ——'s making some remark, "Johnson has said worse things than that"; then, after a short pause, "and *better*." R.'s story of the parson who was called upon suddenly to preach to some invalid establishment; poor, maimed creatures, hardly one of them able to get over a stile; and the only sermon he happened to have with him, and which he preached, was one against *foreign travel*. Grattan's saying to a lady, who asked him what was the subject of some letter he was reading, "It is a secret." "Well, but tell it now." "No; I would trust my life in your hands, but not a secret."

April 2 ... Dined at Lord Lansdowne's. Company: Lord Auckland, Macaulay, Rogers, Schlegel, Charles Murray, &c. Rogers seated next Schlegel[1], and suffering manifest agony from the German's loud voice and unnecessary use of it. Got placed between Lady Lansdowne and Macaulay very agreeably. In quoting Voltaire's "Superflu, chose si necessaire," I remarked that it had been suggested, I thought, by a passage in Pascal's *Lettres Provinciales;* and Macaulay agreed with me, and remembering (as he does everything), repeated the passage.

Had some talk with Schlegel after dinner; asked me, if a man conscientiously, and without any intentional levity, published a book in England expressive of his disbelief in the Scriptures, and giving the reasons of his disbelief, how such a book would be received? Answered, that as to the *book*, I didn't know, but I knew well how the *man* would be received; and I should not like to be in his place. In speaking of Pope, whom I, of course, praised, but whom he seemed not to have much taste for, he exclaimed, "Yes, to be sure, there are some fine things in him; that passage, for instance, 'Upon her neck a sparkling cross she wore,' charming!" So much for the German's appreciation of Pope. Intimated that Goethe was jealous of him in consequence of some Indian

[1] August Wilhelm von Schlegel (1767–1845), the German critic and historian of the drama.

poem that he (Schlegel) wrote or translated. Rogers and I in doubt whether we should go to Lady Grey's or Lord Burghersh's music; decided for the latter. Told me, that on his asking Schlegel, in allusion to Goethe's death, "Are there any German poets now left?" Schlegel blurted out, "*I* am a German poet"; throwing his arms open pompously as he said it. Lord Lansdowne, by the bye, told me a curious mistake Charles Grant had made on his introducing Schlegel to him. Lord L. had told the latter beforehand, that Charles G. was very much versed in Indian learning; and the first thing Schlegel said to him when they were presented to each other was, "On m'a dit, monsieur, que vous vous occupez de la littérature Sanscrite." "Mais toute l'Europe sait cela," answered Grant; thinking that Schlegel had said he was himself so occupied.

Heard an anecdote (this morning I think) from Robinson[1], which is interesting, as showing, what I have never doubted, that poetry is a far more matter-of-fact thing than your people, who are only matter-of-fact, can understand or allow. Goethe told Robinson that his description of the Carnival at Rome, which is accounted one of the most delightful of his writings, had its origin in the following manner. Goethe's lodgings were on the Corso, and being solitary and *ennuyé*, he amused himself by taking notes exactly of all that passed before his eyes during the Carnival; and from these matter-of-fact notes, without any addition from fancy, he afterwards composed his description. Mentioned this to Schlegel to-day, and he confirmed the truth of it.

[1] Crabb Robinson.

April 3 Breakfasted with Rogers. Company: Macaulay, Luttrell, Lord Kerry, and Wishaw.... Luttrell's story of a tailor who used to be seen attending the Greek lectures constantly, and when some one noticed it to him as odd, the tailor saying modestly, that he knew too well what became his station to intrude himself as an auditor on any of those subjects of which from his rank in life he must be supposed to be ignorant; but "really (he added) at a *Greek* lecture I think we are all pretty much on a par."

April 6 Breakfasted at Lord John's. Company: Lady Hardy and one of her daughters, Lord William, Sydney Smith, and Luttrell: Sydney delightful. When the horse guards were passing the windows, said to Lord W., "I suppose now you must feel the same in looking at those that I do in looking at a congregation." Talking of the feelings people must have on going into battle, Lord William appealed to. Said it was, at first, always a very anxious and awful feeling, but soon went off. I mentioned my having been on board a frigate when she was cleared for action; and Luttrell said he had been in the same situation aboard a Post Office packet, and had a musket put into his hands. This set Sydney off on the ingloriousness of such a combat; drawing a penny-post cutlass, and crying, "Freeling for ever!" Spoke of the knowledge sailors have of ships at a great distance; took them off, saying, with a telescope to the eye, "Damn her, she's the 'Delight' laden with tallow."

Sydney highly comical about Sir Henry Halford; his

rout pill, to carry a lady over the night; his parliamentary pill, &c. Never shakes any one by the hand; seizes always the wrist.

Told of Leslie, the Scotch philosopher, once complaining to him that Jeffrey had "damned the North Pole." Leslie had called upon Jeffrey just as the latter was going out riding to explain some point (in an article for the *Edinburgh Review*, I believe) concerning the North Pole; and Jeffrey, who was in a hurry, exclaimed impatiently, as he rode off, "O, damn the North Pole!" This Leslie complained of to Sydney; who entered gravely into his feelings, and told him in confidence, that he himself had once heard Jeffrey "speak disrespectfully of the Equator." Left Lord John's with Sydney and Luttrell; and when we got to Cockspur Street (having laughed all the way) we were all three seized with such convulsions of cachinnation at something (I forget what) which Sydney said, that we were obliged to separate, and reel each his own way with the fit; I thought if any one that knew us happened to be looking, how it would amuse them. Turned back with Sydney to call at the Duke of Northumberland's; left our cards. Told me that he had been knocked down by a coach the other day in crossing the street, and was nearly run over; and that, knowing how much of Lord Grey's patronage had accrued from accidents happening to clergymen, he found himself saying as he came down, "There's a vacancy."

May 12 A letter from Crampton, which Bessy gave me, saying that my darling mother was almost insensible;

but that, as she had recovered from quite as bad a state before, she might now; and entreating me not to stir till I should hear from him again. Resolved to start immediately; but after breakfast my sweet Bessy, after preparing my mind to hear the worst, produced another letter from Peter Leigh, which she had withheld, and which contained the account that all was over (on Wednesday night), and that the funeral was to take place on this very morning (Saturday).

It is now useless, besides being painful, to say what I felt at the event. I had been too well prepared for it to feel anything violent, and the effect it had upon me was rather that of deep and saddening depression, which continued for some days, and seemed more like bodily indisposition than any mental affliction. The fact was too that I *was* ill, whether from the shock at the last I know not. The difference it makes in life to have lost *such* a mother, those only who have had that blessing, and have lost it, can feel: it is like a part of one's life going out of one.

May 23 Received a letter from Captain Marryat[1], the proprietor of the *Metropolitan*, proposing to me a £1000. a year, if I would become editor of the *Metropolitan*, and saying there would be no necessity for my living in town in consequence, as there was a subeditor who would look to all the details. Took time to consider of the proposition, which was one not hastily to be rejected. I had sent up to them the verses to Lady Valletort, and had said that whatever sum they

[1] Frederick Marryat (1792–1848), the novelist.

thought them worth would be very acceptable; in consequence of which Marryat now inclosed me £100., expressing a hope that I would continue my contributions through the next two numbers. Returned him the £100., saying that I could not pledge myself to any further contributions, and that for the verses I had sent a sum in proportion to what Mr Saunders had offered annually would be abundantly sufficient.

May 24 to 26 From some late letters of Lady Morgan on the subject of the *Metropolitan*, I had been led to believe that Campbell meant to give up the editorship of the magazine, which belief alone could have induced me to enter into any negotiations on the subject. Finding, however, from Marryat that Campbell was still to continue in the concern, I felt that my engaging as editor would look like forcing myself into his shoes; and therefore wrote to decline the proposition, saying, that "though I should consider it an honour to *succeed* Campbell, I could not possibly think of *supplanting* him."

May 27 Another offer from Marryat, which he said he could not help making, though with but little hope of my accepting it; and this was £500. a year for contributions as often as it might suit me to give them, and only stipulating that for each of the three next numbers I should give them something. This I felt was too liberal an offer and too convenient to me in my present circumstances to refuse, though hating the thing most heartily, and still feeling it to be a sort of degradation of literature. I wrote to him to say that

I should act unfairly, both by him and myself, were I, without the consideration, to reject an offer so handsome, and that, therefore, I should turn the matter over in my mind and let him know my determination in a day or two.

May 30 Wrote to Marryat, to say I accepted his offer for one year.

June 1 *to* 16 Much annoyed and disgusted on receiving the new number of the *Metropolitan* (that which contains my verses to Lady Valletort) to see some ribald attacks upon Rogers in it, and also some vulgar trash about myself. The latter I didn't care a pin about, but the stuff against Rogers, appearing in a work with which my name will now be connected, annoyed me exceedingly and gave me the first specimen of the sort of tarnish one must expect by such contact. Wrote to Captain Marryat to say that I really must pause here, and ask leave to be off my bargain, if there could be the slightest risk of any repetition of such disreputable attacks. Received a very gentlemanlike answer from Marryat, to say that he was as much shocked as I had been to see the passages about Rogers; and that I might depend upon nothing of the kind being ever again suffered to appear.

September 28 Walked home; Rogers with me great part of the way. Told a story of a young girl who had been sacristine (query, are there female sacristines?) in a convent, and conducted herself most innocently and industriously; till having her imagination inflamed by the searching questions of the confessor, she left her situation and abandoned herself to a licentious life. Her becoming weary of it and repenting, and returning to the neighbourhood of the convent; where some woman, a stranger to her, seeing her fatigue and distress, asks her to take refreshment. The girl inquiring about the convent and asking who was now sacristine of it; and the woman answering, "Antonia" (the girl's own name), and adding, "The same who has been sacristine for some years; a very good and pious girl." The girl's amazement; and her having a dream that night, in which the Virgin Mary appeared to her and said, that in consideration of her previous goodness and innocence, and the prospect of her repentance, she herself had acted as sacristine for her ever since her fall, and that she might now resume her place without tarnish, and become again worthy of her former character. R. said, that on mentioning this story (which W. Irving had told him) to Lady Holland, she remembered having read it somewhere, and sending her page for a volume of Le Grand's *Fabliaux*, they found it[1].

October 8 ... Thought of calling at Rogers's, on the chance of his not having yet gone to Broadstairs: found that he was not to go till morning and would dine at home, alone; so took my seat and waited his return. A most agreeable *tête-à-tête* dinner and evening. Spoke of poor Mackintosh[2]; said he had sacrificed himself to conversation; that he read for it, thought for it, and

[1] It has turned up since in John Davidson's *Ballad of a Nun*.
[2] Mackintosh had recently died.

gave up future fame for it. Told an anecdote of the
Empress Catherine, which Lord St Helens had related
to him. At one of her private parties, when she was as
usual walking about from card-table to card-table looking
at the players, she suddenly rang the bell for her page,
but he did not come; she looked agitated and impatient, and rang again, but still no page appeared. At
length she left the room, and did not again return; and
conjecture was of course busy as to what might be the
fate of the inattentive page. Shortly after, however,
some one having occasion to go into the ante-chamber
of the pages, found a party of them at cards, and the
Empress seated playing along with them. The fact was,
she had found that the page she rung for was so interested
in the game he was engaged in, that he could not leave
it to attend to her summons; and accordingly she had
quietly taken his hand for him, to play it out, while he
went on the errand. So meekly can they who have the
power of life and death over those around them sometimes deal with their slaves! Lord St Helens himself
was one of the Empress's company on the occasion.

October 12 Went to the meeting at Murray's relative
to the subscription for Sir W. Scott. Found there Scott
of Harden, Sir Coutts Trotter, Pusey, Hay, and one
or two more. The object was to raise a sum for the
purchase of Abbotsford. A statement of the amount
of property left by him, how disposed of, and how en-
cumbered, was laid before us. Abbotsford itself, it appeared, was not worth at the utmost £600. a year; and
it would take that sum at least to keep it up, the very

window-tax absorbing a good part of it. Though Scott was insolvent (not, of course, knowing that he was so) at the time when he settled Abbotsford on his son's wife, it appears that the settlement is not (as it would have been in other cases) null; as, Mrs Scott's fortune (£60,000.) having been advanced on the faith of that settlement, her claim takes precedence of that of the creditors. Letters were read from Scotland requesting that we should merge our object in theirs and subscribe for the monument: as if the most solid monument, and the most welcome (if I may say so) to the spirit of Scott himself, would not be the gift from the country to his family of the place which will be for ever connected with his name. I saw plainly that there was but little hope of our object being attained; and fear much that even Party has a good deal to do with the coldness if not disinclination manifested towards it, as if forgetting that Scott was a man of mankind, and one that ought not to be measured within the small and wretched circumference of Party.

August 4 Drove to Regent's Park; Rogers told of Coleridge riding about in a strange shabby dress, with I forget whom at Keswick, and on some company approaching them, Coleridge offered to fall behind and pass for his companion's servant. "No," said the other, "I am proud of you as a friend; but, I must say, I should be ashamed of you as a servant."

October 16 Some agreeable conversation after breakfast with Smith and Lord Lansdowne. In talking of

O'Connell, of the mixture there is in him of high and low, formidable and contemptible, mighty and mean, Smith summed up all by saying, "The only way to deal with such a man is to hang him up and erect a statue to him under his gallows." This *balancing* of the account is admirable. Told of Lord Camelford taking an old fiddler with him to Tom's (a place where, during the times of Jacobinism, the Radical fellows used to assemble at night), and having planted his musician in a corner, taking his seat by him and saying, "There, now play God save the King." In a small minority there was on one occasion for peace, upon a question moved by Lord Grey, the name of Lord Camelford was, to the astonishment of everybody, found among the peace-seekers; but it turned out that he had, for some offence, challenged a German officer who refused to fight him till *after* the war, and he therefore felt himself bound, in spite of his political opinions, to vote for peace.

November 2 Some conversation after breakfast in the library (of Holland House). Found them inclined to decry Wordsworth, and said what I thought of his great powers, and of the injustice this age does him. "Ah, this is talking for candour," said Lady Holland. Soon after, taking a volume of Crabbe from one of the shelves, Lord Melbourne said, "I see there is a new edition of Crabbe coming out; it is a good thing when these authors die, for then one gets their works, and has done with them." Though this sounds insolent when written, it was said with so joyous and jovial an air, followed by that scarcely human though cheerful laugh of Lord Melbourne's, with his ejaculations "Eh! eh!" interposed at every burst, that it was impossible not to enjoy it as much as himself.

November 9 Had Tom out from the Charter House, and walked about with him a little. Dined at Lockhart's. Had asked Murray whether Lockhart would have any objection to my taking Tom with me, as I was, in a degree, pledged to him on Saturdays, and Lockhart's note, in answer, was, very good-humouredly, "Surely we shall be delighted to have Tom Moore the younger, as well as Tom Brown the younger." Would not have asked this, however, had I known it was a dinner of company, which it turned out to be. Was too far from Coleridge, during dinner, to hear more than the continual drawl of his preachment; moved up to him, however, when the ladies had retired. His subject chiefly Irving and religion; is employed himself, it seems, in writing on Daniel and the Revelations, and his notions on the subject, as far as they were at all intelligible, appeared to be a strange mixture of rationalism and mysticism. Thus, with the rationalists, he pronounced the gift of tongues to have been nothing more than scholarship or a knowledge of different languages; said that this was the opinion of Erasmus, as may be deduced from his referring to Plato's *Timæus* on the subject. (Must see to this.) Gave an account of his efforts to bring Irving to some sort of rationality on these subjects, to "steady him," as he expressed it; but his efforts all unsuccessful, and, after many conversations between them, Irving confessed that the only effect of all that Coleridge had said was "to *stun*" him,—an effect I can well conceive, from my own short experiment of the operation.

Repeated two or three short pieces of poetry he had written lately, one an epitaph on himself; all very striking, and in the same mystical religious style as his conversation. A large addition to the party in the evening, and music. Duets by Mrs Macleod and her sister, which brought back sadly to my memory an evening of the same kind, in this same room, with poor Sir Walter Scott, before he went abroad for his health. One of the duets, in which the voices rose alternately above each other, Coleridge said reminded him of *arabesques*. With my singing he seemed really much pleased, and spoke eloquently of the perfect union (as he was pleased to say) of poetry and music which it exhibited: "The music, like the honeysuckle round the stem, twining round the meaning, and at last overtopping it." In the course of his oratory to-day Coleridge said, "It is in fact the greatest mistake in the world to rest the authority of an ancient church upon any other basis than tradition"; upon which Dr Ferguson turning round to me said, "That falls in with *your* views, Mr Moore."

November 14 Had received a note from Barnes to ask me to go with him and Mrs Barnes to Walter's place near Reading; answered that I would, if possible, follow them thither. A note from Sydney Smith, fixing to call upon me, and containing a bill of fare which he has suggested to Mrs Longman as proper for her entomological guests, to-day, Spence and Kirby; "to wit, flea-patés, earthworms on toast, caterpillars crawling in cream and removing themselves," &c. &c. Called upon me in a hackney coach.... Smith said, that where he felt he had a good and just claim, he considered it always a duty to himself and family to ask, and not to let the world have to say, "If he *did* fall into adversity, that was his own fault." What he had hitherto done was all by his own exertions, as neither himself nor any of his brothers had received a shilling from their father. In talking of the fun he had had in the early times of the *Edinburgh Review*, mentioned an article on Ritson, which he and Brougham had written together; and one instance of their joint contribution which he gave me was as follows: "We take for granted (wrote Brougham) that Mr Ritson supposes Providence to have had some share in producing him—though for what inscrutable purposes (added Sydney) we profess ourselves unable to conjecture." The road up to Longmans being rather awkward, we had desired the hackney coachman to wait for us at the bottom. "It would never do (said S.) when your Memoirs come to be written to have it said, 'He went out to dine at the house of the respectable publishers, Longman and Co., and, being overturned on his way back, was crushed to death by a large clergyman.'"

January 4 Went to the Hollands' (Burlington Street), having received a very kind note from my Lady yesterday. Found only Lord Melbourne, and soon after came Talleyrand, who was full of the King's speech. Talked of Champfort; said he was one of those "qui dansent toujours, et ne peuvent pas marcher"; that he was an enemy to *l'état social*; his talent was to *ramasser*. Wits of former times used to *gaspiller*, but our more modern ones "ramassent et ne gaspillent pas." It appears that Talleyrand is constantly at the Hollands. "You are sure to be Talleyranded there," said Sydney Smith: a good verb.

August 11 Dined at Lady Blessington's. Company: D'Orsay as master of the house, John Ponsonby, Willis the American, Count Pahlen (whom I saw a good deal of when he was formerly in London, and liked), Fonblanque, the editor of *The Examiner*, and a foreigner, whose name I forget. Sat next to Fonblanque, and was glad of the opportunity of knowing him. A clever fellow certainly, and with great powers occasionally as a writer. Got on very well together. Broached to him my notions (long entertained by me) respecting the ruinous effects to literature likely to arise from the boasted diffusion of education; the lowering of the standard that must necessarily arise from the extending of the circle of judges; from letting the mob in to vote, particularly at a period when the *market* is such an object to authors. Those "who live to please must please to live," and most will write down to the lowered standard. All the great things in literature have been achieved when the readers were few; "fit audience find and few." In the best days of English genius, what a comparatively small circle sat in judgment! In the Italian Republics, in old Greece, the dispensers of fame were a select body, and the consequence was a high standard of taste. Touched upon some of these points to Fonblanque, and he seemed not indisposed to agree with me: observing that certainly the present appearances in the world of literature looked very like a confirmation of my views.

August 12 Breakfasted at home; made some calls; at Shee's. Showed me a new work, *Naval Recollections,* in which there is mention of me, and such as pleases me not a little. The author, it appears, was midshipman on board the "Phaeton" frigate in which I went to America, and describes the regret of the officers of the gun-room when I quitted the ship, adding some kind things about their feelings towards me, which I had great pleasure in reading. To have left such an impression upon honest, hearty, unaffected fellows like those of the gun-room of the "Phaeton," is not a little flattering to me. I remember the first lieutenant saying to me, after we had become intimate, "I thought you, the first day you came aboard, the damnedest conceited little fellow I ever saw, with your glass cocked up to your eye"; and then he mimicked the manner in which I made my first appearance.

Went to the Hollands, where I found a scene that would rather have alarmed, I think, a Tory of the full dress school. There was the Chancellor in his black frock coat and black cravat; while upon the sofa lay stretched the Prime Minister, also in frock and boots, and with his legs cocked up on one of Lady Holland's fine chairs. Beside him sat Lord Holland, and at some distance from this group was my Lady herself, seated at a table with Talleyrand, and occupying him in conversation to divert his attention from the Ministerial confab at the sofa. Joined these two, being the first time that I was ever regularly introduced to Talleyrand. Was very civil; said Mr Moore was "très connu en France." A book lying upon the table which Lady H. had been recommended, and had sent to Paris for it, but would not now read it. This book was Leroy's *Lettres Philosophiques sur l'Intelligence et la Perfectibilité des Animaux*. Talleyrand strongly advised her to read it, and said (in French, for he never speaks English), "Lend it to Mr Moore, and I am sure, after he has read it, he will be of my opinion about it. I remember, when a young man, going *à la chasse* with that Monsieur Leroy, who was Lieutenant des Chasses du Parc de Versailles; and the Abbé Condillac was also of the party."

September 16 Sydney at breakfast made me actually cry with laughing. I was obliged to start up from the table. In talking of the intelligence and concert which birds have among each other, cranes and crows, &c., showing that they must have some means of communicating their thoughts, he said, "I dare say they make the same remark of us. That old fat crow there (meaning himself) what a prodigious noise he is making! I have no doubt he has some power of communicating," &c. &c. After pursuing this idea comically for some time he added, "But we have the advantage of them; they can't put us into pies as we do them; legs sticking up

out of the crust," &c. &c. The acting of all this makes
two-thirds of the fun of it; the quickness, the buoyancy,
the self-enjoying laugh. Talking of Bayle after breakfast, was surprised at Sydney's low opinion of him. Said
that you found everything in Bayle but the thing you
wanted to find.

Walked with him about the grounds; his conversation, as is usually the case in a *tête-à-tête*, grave and
sensible. Discussed O'Connell's character, and though,
for the pleasure of the argument (which Sydney delights
in) questioning most of my opinions, yet upon the whole
I found he agreed with my views. Mentioned his first
interview with Dan, who had called upon him, and he
went to return the visit. Found some people there, to
whom O'Connell presented him, saying, "Allow me
to introduce to you the ancient and amusing defender
of our faith"; on which Sydney laughingly interrupted
him, saying, "Of your *cause*, if you please, *not* of your
faith."

September 18 At breakfast Sydney enumerated and
acted the different sorts of hand-shaking there are to be
met with in society. The *digitory* or one finger, ex-
emplified in Brougham, who puts forth his fore-finger,
and says, with his strong northern accent, "How *arrre*
you?" The *sepulchral* or *mortemain*, which was
Mackintosh's manner, laying his open hand flat and
coldly against yours. The *high official*, the Archbishop
of York's, who carries your hand aloft on a level with
his forehead. The *rural* or *vigorous* shake, &c. &c. In
talking of the remarkable fact that women in general

bear pain much better than men, I said that allowing
everything that could be claimed for the superior
patience and self-command of women, still the main
solution of their enduring pain better than men was their
having less physical sensibility. This theory of mine
was immediately exclaimed against (as it always is whenever I sport it) as disparaging, ungenerous, unfounded,
&c. &c. I offered to put it to the test by bringing in a
hot tea-pot, which I would answer for the ladies of
the party being able to hold for a much longer time
than the men. This set Sydney off most comically,
upon my cruelty to the female part of the creation, and
the practice I had in such experiments. " He has been
all his life (he said) trying the sex with hot tea-pots;
the burning ploughshare was nothing to it. I think I
hear his terrific tone in a *tête-à-tête*. 'Bring a tea-pot.'"

February 20 After some hours' work, set off westward.
Wrote my letters at Brookes's, and from thence to
Rogers's; a good speculation, as it turned out. His
servant, on opening the door, asked eagerly, "Are you
come to dine here, Sir? Mr Wordsworth is coming."
Found that Rogers, though engaged out himself, had
asked Wordsworth and his wife, who are just arrived
in town, to dinner. Mrs Wordsworth not well enough
to come, but Rogers, W., and myself sat down to
dinner at half past five, and our host having done the
honours of the table to us till near seven o'clock, went
off to his other engagement and left us *tête-à-tête*.

My companion, according to his usual fashion, very
soliloquacious, but saying much, of course, that was

interesting to hear. In one of my after-dinner conversations with the people of the Row lately, they had told me that they were about to publish a new volume of poems for Wordsworth, and that an interest was evidently excited by their announcement, which showed that the public were still alive to the claims of good poetry. Then they expressed a strong wish that I would undertake a new poem; and on my saying, that I doubted much the power of any poet at this moment to make an impression upon the public, dosed as they had been with rhymes so *usque ad nauseum*, they all agreed, to my surprise, in declaring that a poem from me would be as successful a speculation just now as any they could name, and all concurred in urging me to think of it. This, of course, was agreeable to me to hear; though I confess I am not the less sceptical as to the soundness of their opinion, men of business being (from their speculation, I suppose,) the greatest of all castle-builders: we poets are nothing to them. Told as much of this to Wordsworth as he himself was concerned in, sinking or softening down my own share in the honour, though Rogers (who was by part of the time) *would* try and fasten upon me some little self-ostentation on the subject. This led to Wordsworth's telling me, what certainly is no small disgrace to the taste of the English public, of the very limited sale of his works, and the very scanty sum, on the whole, which he had received for them, not more, I think, than about a thousand pounds in all. I dare say I must have made by my writings at least twenty times that sum; but then I have written twenty times as much, such as it is. In giving me an account of the sort of society he has in his neighbourhood in the country, and saying that he rarely went out to dinner, he gave a very intelligible picture of the sort of thing it must be when he *does* go out. "The conversation," he said, "may be called *catechetical;* for, as they do me the honour to wish to know my opinions on the different subjects, they ask me questions, and I am induced to answer them at great length till I become quite tired." And so he does, I'll warrant him; nor is it possible, indeed, to edge in a word, at least in a *tête-à-tête*, till he *does* get tired. I was, however, very well pleased to be a listener.

Spoke of the immense time it took him to write even the shortest copy of verses,—sometimes whole weeks employed in shaping two or three lines, before he can satisfy himself with their structure. Attributed much of this to the unmanageableness of the English as a poetical language: contrasted it with the Italian in this respect, and repeated a stanza of Tasso, to show how naturally the words fell into music of themselves. It was one where the double rhymes, "ella," "nella," "quella," occurred, which he compared with the meagre and harsh English words "she," "that," "this," &c. &c. Thought, however, that, on the whole, there were advantages in having a rugged language to deal with; as in struggling with words one was led to give birth to and dwell upon thoughts, while, on the contrary, an easy and mellifluous language was apt to tempt, by its facility, into negligence, and to lead the poet to substitute music for thought. I do not give these as at all *his words*, but rather my deductions from his sayings than what he actually said. Talked of Coleridge, and praised him, not merely as a poet, but as a man, to a degree which I could not listen to without putting in my protest. Hinted something of this in reply to Wordsworth's praises, and adverted to Southey's opinion of him, as expressed in a letter to Bowles, (saying, if I recollect right, that he was "lamented by few, and regretted by none,") but Wordsworth continued his eulogium. Defended Coleridge's desertion of his family on the grounds of incompatibility, &c., between him and Mrs Coleridge: said that Southey took a "rigid view" of the whole matter; and, in short, made out as poor a case for his brother bard (and proser), as any opponent of the latter could well desire.

In speaking of Byron's attacks upon himself, seemed to think they all originated in something Rogers told Byron of a letter written by him (Wordsworth) to a lady who applied to him for contributions to some miscellany. Being in a little fit of abstraction at the moment, I did not well attend to the particulars of this anecdote; but it seemed to imply such gratuitous mischief-making on the part of Rogers, that, imperfectly as I had collected the facts, I pronounced at once that Wordsworth must have been misinformed on the subject. He said he would ask Rogers about it, and I intended to do the same, but it went out of my mind. In remarking upon the causes of an author's popularity (with reference to his own failure, as he thought, in that respect), he mentioned, as one of them, the frequent occurrence of quotable passages,—of lines that dwelt in people's memories, and passed into general circulation. This, he paid me the compliment of saying, was the case very much with my writings; but the tribute was a very equivocal one, as he intimated that he did not consider it to be the case with his own,—and one knows well what he considers the standard of perfection. I did not like to appear to bandy compliments, otherwise I could have contradicted his notion, that there were not many lines of his widely and popularly remembered. And here I do not allude to those which are remembered only to be laughed at, such as—

> I've measured it from side to side,
> 'Tis three feet long and two feet wide;

or the doggerel of *Peter Bell*, &c. &c., but to such touching things as, "Thoughts that lie too deep for tears," and the imaginative line, "Whose dwelling is the light of setting suns," as well as several others of the same character that have spread beyond the circle of his devoted admirers, and become universally known. On the subject of Coleridge, as a writer, Wordsworth gave it as his opinion (strangely, I think) that his prose would live and deserve to live; while, of his poetry, he thought by no means so highly. I had mentioned the *Genevieve* as a beautiful thing, but to this he objected: there was too much of the sensual in it.

August 7 To Liverpool by the railroad; a grand mode of travelling, though, as we were told, ours was but a poor specimen of it, as we took an hour and a half to do the thirty-two miles, which rarely requires more than an hour and a quarter or twenty minutes. The motion so easy that I found I could write without any difficulty *chemin faisant*.

August 26 [IN IRELAND] After breakfast set off for Wexford in a chaise and four, Boyse thinking we should have full time for my visit to the corn-market (an old recollection of mine) before we proceeded to our Banmow friends. The weather still most prosperous. While horses were getting ready, Boyse and I walked to the corn-market.

While I was looking at this locality, a few persons had begun to collect around me, and some old women (entering into my feelings) ran before me to the wretched house I was in search of (which is now a small pot-house), crying out, "Here, sir, this is the very house where your grandmother lived. Lord be merciful to her!" Of the grand*mother* I have no knowledge, for she died long before my youthful visit here; but I have a pretty clear recollection of little old Tom Codd, my grandfather, as well of some sort of weaving machinery in the room up-stairs. My mother used to say he was a provision merchant, which sounded well, and I have no doubt he may have been concerned in that trade, but I suspect that he was also a weaver. Nothing, at all events, could be more humble and mean that the little low house which still remains to tell of his whereabouts; and it shows how independent Nature is of mere localities that one of the noblest-minded, as well as most warm-hearted, of all God's creatures (that ever it has been my lot to know) was born under that lowly roof.

Wrote a hasty letter to my sweet Bess before we started, and then set off in gay style, rosettes at the ears of the horses (four very dashing posters), cockades in the hats of the boys, &c. Several groups whom we saw in the fields on our way, too hard at work at the harvest to join our sport, stood up and cheered us heartily as we passed. As we approached Banmow, Boyse was evidently anxious lest the doubt that had existed as to my time and way of coming might have caused a dispersion of the multitude, and so produce a failure in the effect of the cavalcade. We now saw at a distance a party of horsemen on the look-out for us, bearing green banners, and surrounded by people on foot. This party, which turned out to be a mere detachment from the main body, now proceeded in advance of us, and after a short time we came in sight of the great multitude—chiefly on foot, but as we passed along we found numbers of carriages of different kinds, filled with ladies, drawn up on each side of the road, which, after we had passed them, fell into the line and followed in procession. When we arrived at the first triumphal arch, there was the decorated car and my Nine Muses, some of them remarkably pretty girls, particularly the one who placed the crown on my head; and after we had proceeded a little way, seeing how much they were pressed by the crowd, I made her and two of her companions get up on the car behind me. As the whole affair has been described in print (diffusely and enthusiastically enough, Heaven knows!), I shall not here waste time and words upon it, though certainly it would be difficult to say too much of the warmth and cordiality of feeling evinced by the whole assemblage, as well as the quickness and intelligence with which the very lowest of them entered into the whole spirit of the ceremony. In advance of the car was a band of amateur musicians, smart young fellows, in a uniform of blue jackets, caps, and white trousers, who, whenever we stopped at the arches erected along the road, played some of the most popular Irish Melodies, and likewise, more than once, an air that has been adapted to Byron's *Here's a health to thee, Tom Moore*. As we proceeded slowly along, I said to my pretty Muse behind me, "This is a long journey for you." "Oh, sir!" she exclaimed, with a sweetness and kindness of look not to be found in more artificial life, "I wish it was more than three hundred miles." It is curious, and not easy, perhaps, to be accounted for, that as I passed along in all this triumph, with so many cordial and sweet faces turned towards me, a feeling of deep sadness came more than once over my heart. Whether it might not have been some of the Irish airs they played that called up mournful associations connected with the *reverse* of all this smiling picture, I know not, but so it was.

When we arrived in front of the Graigue House, the speeches from Boyse and myself (as reported) took place; Boyse very eloquent, and evidently in high favour with the people. I then went with him to his new house, or rather the few fragments of the old one he has left standing; the offices being all that are as yet built of the new. He had told me before I came that I was literally to dine in one cock-loft and sleep in another; but I found he had given me up his own bedroom, which was on the ground-floor, and left standing quite alone, all around it having been thrown down. It was, however, made very comfortable by dint of green baize curtains, &c. &c. Was now introduced to his mother, a very fine handsome old lady, about eighty-one or so; and his maiden sister, a nice, intelligent, and very amiable person; and likewise a little round, joyous girl, their niece, between fourteen and fifteen years old, who, I was told, could not conceive what sort of a thing a *bard* was, never having seen one, and had been, accordingly, most anxious for my arrival. Old Mr Boyse (about the same age as the mother) was confined to his bed with illness, and I did not see him all the time I remained. Before dinner Miss Boyse drove me in her pony chaise to see the grounds of the Graigue House, a new property they have lately purchased, and the same that Boyse wrote last summer to offer to me and my family in case I should wish for a quiet retreat for two or three months. We fancied it, from his description to be a small cottage overhanging the sea; but it is, in fact, a large house with extensive pleasure-grounds, and the walk to the sea (a sort of garden wall all along) is not less, I should think, than three-quarters of a mile in length. Miss Boyse, her niece, and I took this walk after dinner, and the open breathing-space over the sea felt highly refreshing.

August 27 Prepared, while dressing, my short answer to the deputations which, I understood, were to wait upon me. Found that there had been bonfires lighted in various directions during the night. Proceeded towards twelve o'clock to Graigue, where we found a great part of the crowd of yesterday reassembled in their gayest trim, this day being devoted to a *fête* for the lads and lasses on the green. Went through my reception of the various addresses very successfully, and (as Boyse told me afterwards) spoke much louder and less *Englishly* than I did the day before. I find that the English accent (which I always had, by the by, never having, at any time of my life, spoken with much brogue,) is not liked by the genuine *Pats*. Among other introductions I was presented in form to the reverend president of Peter's College and a number of Catholic clergymen who accompanied him. Just as I was approaching this reverend body, I saw among the groups that lined the way, my pretty Muse of yesterday, and her young companions, still arrayed in their green wreaths and gowns. Flesh and blood could not resist the impulse of stopping a minute to shake hands with a few of them, which I did most heartily, to the great amusement of all around, not excepting the reverend president himself, who had been approaching me with a grave face when I was thus interrupted; and who, immediately joining in the laugh, said, very good humouredly, "I like to see *character* display itself."

After these ceremonies were over, Boyse took me in his curricle to see some points of view in his immediate neighbourhood; not the most agreeable part of our operations, as I saw he was not much in the habit of driving, and one of the horses was what is called "an awkward customer." After driving about a little (the roads being like avenues, and everything, in short, wearing a face of comfort and prosperity) we went to the house of an honest Quaker, Mr Elly, one of those most zealous, Boyse told me, in organising all the preparations for my reception. There we found a large party assembled, and a *déjeûner* prepared; the young amateur band being in attendance, and playing occasionally my songs. The situation of the villa, commanding a view of the Tintern shore, appeared to me, except for the want of trees, very beautiful, and a large flag waving from the top of the house displayed the words, "Erin go bragh, and Tom Moore for ever." The *déjeûner* (*i.e.* the eating part of it) was provided, ungallantly enough, for the males alone; an anomaly, of which I had already witnessed another instance at the Zoological Gardens, in Dublin, where it was not till after the men had feasted that the ladies were admitted into the gardens. Dined, as the day before, with Boyse's family party, and all went afterwards to the *fête* at Graigue, where we found them in high dance and glee. The music being very inspiring, I took out my young Muse (Boyse having, in spite of his lameness, turned out with another), and after dancing down a few couples, surrendered her (very *unwillingly*, I own) to her former partner. Should have liked exceedingly a little more of the fun, but thought it better, on every account, to stop where I did. Among other reasons, I feared that Boyse might think it necessary to go on as long as *I* did.

Two very nice Quaker young women were among the crowd looking at the dancing, and as I had taken some pains to place them where they could have a good view, one of them, encouraged by this attention, said to me, very modestly, "if it would not be asking too much, I should like to have two lines of thine with thy name to them." Promised, of course, that she should have them. In the course of the evening a green balloon was seen ascending above the dancers' heads, with "Welcome, Tom Moore," upon it. When it grew dusk, Miss Boyse, her niece, and myself came away, leaving the dancers to keep up the *fête*, as they did, I believe, till near morning. Wishing for a solitary walk to the sea, I asked Miss Boyse to direct me to the path we had taken the evening before; but with my usual confusion as to localities, I missed the right way, and could find nothing but those smooth roads which I had admired so much in the morning, but felt *now* rather inclined to anathematise, having seldom ever thirsted more keenly for actual beverage than I did at that moment for a draught of the fresh sea air.

August 30 A charming letter from my sweet admirable Bessy about the new accession to our means, which made me by turns laugh and weep, being, as I told her in my answer, almost the counterpart of Dr Pangloss's

> I often wished that I had clear,
> For life three hundred pounds a year.

I cannot refrain from copying a passage or two, here and there, from her letter, which she wrote before mine, conveying the intelligence of the grant, reached her.

"Sloperton, Tuesday night.

"My dearest Tom,—Can it *really* be true that you have a pension of £300. a year? Mrs., Mr., two

Misses, and young Longman were here to-day, and tell me it is really the case, and that they have seen it in two papers. Should it turn out true, I know not how we can be thankful enough to those who gave it, or to a Higher Power. The Longmans were very kind and nice, and so was *I*, and I invited them *all five* to come at some future time. At present, I can think of nothing but £300. a year, and dear Russell jumps and claps his hands with joy. Tom is at Devizes.... If the story is true of the £300., pray give dear Ellen twenty pounds, and *insist* on her drinking five pounds worth of wine *yearly*, to be paid out of the £300. I have been obliged, by the by, to get five pounds to send. to —— ... Three hundred a year, how delightful! But I have my fears that it is only a castle in the air. I am sure I shall dream of it; and so I will go to bed, that I may have this pleasure *at least*; for I expect the morning will throw down my castle."

"Wednesday morning.

"Is it true? I am in a fever of hope and anxiety, and feel very oddly. No one to talk to but sweet Bess, who says, 'Now, Papa will not have to work so hard, and will be able to go out a little.'...

"You say I am so 'nice and comical' about the money. Now you are much more so (leaving out the 'nice'), for you have forgotten to send the cheque you promised. But I can wait with patience, for no one teases me. Only I want to have a few little things ready to welcome you home, which I like to pay for. How you will ever enjoy this quiet every-day sort of stillness, after your late reception, I hardly know. I begin to want you very much; for though the boys are darlings, there is still... How I wish I had wings, for then I would be at Wexford as soon as you, and surprise your new friends. I am so glad you have seen the Gonnes; I know they are quite delighted at your attention. Mr Benett called the other day on my sons.

"N.B. If this good news be true, it will make a great difference in my *eating*. I shall then indulge in butter to potatoes. *Mind* you do not tell this piece of gluttony to *any* one."

December 18 To Bowood to dinner. Company: the Joys, Mrs Brystock and daughter, the Bowleses, &c. Among his multifarious quotations, Joy brought out one from Shakspeare, which struck both Lord Lansdowne and myself from the force and pregnancy of its meaning:

> Now whether it be
> Bestial oblivion, or some *craven scruple*,
> *Of thinking too precisely on the event,*—
> A thought which, quarter'd, hath but one part wisdom,
> And ever three parts coward.

On my remarking that if ever mortal man could be said to be *inspired*, it was Shakspeare; and that he alone of all writers, seemed to have the power of transmigrating, as it were, into every other class and condition of men, and thinking and speaking as they would do under every possible change of feeling and circumstances, Lord Lansdowne expressed himself delighted to hear me speak thus, as he had been under the impression that I was inclined to underrate Shakespeare; and recollected well some friend of mine saying to him, "How odd it is that Moore should think so slightingly of Shakspeare!" This most flagrant misrepresentation of my opinions must have arisen, I think (as I now told him), from some confusion between me and Byron, who *did* affect, very unworthily of himself, to make light of Shakspeare: and, on one occasion, I recollect, said to me, "Well, after all, Tom, don't you think Shakspeare was somewhat of a *humbug*?"

March 6 Dined at Miss Rogers's, R., and I, and Sydney going there together. Company: the Hollands, the Langdales, Lady Davy, Surgeon Travers, and Rogers's nephew. Sydney highly amusing in the evening. His description of the *dining* process, by which people in London extract all they can from new literary lions, was irresistibly comic. "Here's a new man of genius arrived; put on the stew-pan: fry away; we'll soon get it all out of him." On this and one or two other topics, he set off in a style that kept us all in roars of laughter.

April 5 Arrived in Paternoster Row between nine and ten. Rees, by the by, is about to quit the firm, and Tom Longman, the eldest son, who succeeds to his place, has been for some time past my chief business correspondent. A great dinner at the Row, for which I had been secured before I came up; and not a bad thing to start with, as the company consisted of Sydney Smith, Canon Tate (a regular *Princeps Editio* old fellow, whom I had never met with before), Merivale, Dionysius the Tyrant, M'Culloch, and Mr Hayward, the translator of *Faust*. Sydney most rampantly facetious; his whole manner and talk forming a most amusing contrast to the Parson Adams-like simplicity and middle-aged lore of his brother canon, Tate, whom I sat next, and who, between the volleys of Sydney's jokes, was talking to me of "that charming letter written by Vossius to Casaubon," and "the trick played by that rogue Muretus upon Scaliger." *Apropos* of this trick (which was the imposing upon Scaliger, as ancient, some Latin verses written by himself, and which of course Scaliger never forgave), I took occasion to mention that I had often thought of writing a "History of celebrated Forgeries," or rather had thought what a good subject it would be for any person who had time and learning enough to undertake it. The great variety of topic it would embrace; first, the *historical* forgers, Philo of Byblos, Annius of Viterbo, Hector Boece, Geoffrey of Monmouth, &c. Then the *ecclesiastical* impostures, such as the numerous false gospels, &c.; then the *literary* including that of "the rogue Muretus," that of Jortin, "Quæ te sub tenerâ," &c. (which took in, not designedly, however, the learned Gruter), and so on to Chatterton, Lauder, and lastly, Ireland. Conversation turned on Boz, the new comic writer. Was sorry to hear Sydney cry him down, and evidently without having given him a fair trial; whereas, to me it appears one of the few proofs of good taste that "the masses," as they are called, have yet given, there being some as nice humour and fun in the *Pickwick Papers* as in any work I have seen in our day. Hayward, the only one of the party that stood by me in this opinion, engaged me for a dinner (at his chambers) on Thursday next.

August 8 Dined with Rogers to go to the Opera. Party at dinner: Wordsworth and Miss Rogers. A good deal from Wordsworth about his continental tour. In talking of travelling in England, said that he used always to travel on the top of the coach, and still prefers it. Has got at different times subjects for poems by travelling thus. A story he has told in verse (which I have never seen) of two brothers parting on the top of a hill (to go to different regions of the globe), and walking silently down the opposite sides of the hill, was, he said, communicated to him by a fellow traveller outside a coach. Also another story about a peat hill which had been preserved with great care, by a fond father, after the death of the youth who had heaped it up.

August 10 Dinner at Rogers's. Almost over when I arrived. Company: Wordsworth, Landseer, Taylor, and Miss R. A good deal of talk about Campbell's poetry, which they were all much disposed to carp at and depreciate, more particularly Wordsworth. I remarked that Campbell's lesser poems, his sea odes, &c., bid far more fair, I thought, for immortality than almost any of the lyrics of the present day; on which they all began to pick holes in some of the most beautiful of these things. "Every sod beneath their feet shall be a soldier's sepulchre."[1] A *sod* being a sepulchre! (this, perhaps, *is* open to objection). The "meteor flag braving the battle and the *breeze*," another of the things they

[1] I have heard that the word was originally "cemetery." [Lord John Russell's Note.]

objected to. Then his "angels' visits, few and far between," was borrowed from Blair, who says:
> Or, if it did, its visits,
> Like those of angels, short and far between.

Taylor remarked that "The coming events cast their shadows before" was also borrowed, but did not so well make out his case. "Iberian were his boots," another of the blots they hit: altogether very perverse industry.

In talking of letter-writing this evening, and referring to what Tucker has told of Jefferson's sacrifice of his time to correspondence, Wordsworth said that for his own part, such was his horror of having his letters *preserved*, that in order to guard against it, he always took pains to make them as bad and dull as possible.

September 24 Bentley and Moran to breakfast. Bentley full of impatience and ardour for something of mine to publish,—a light Eastern tale, in three volumes. Scene, Circassia; events, founded on the struggle of that people against Russia, and price £1500., with two-thirds of the copyright my own. After we had lunched I walked them over to Spye Park, the day being delicious. Bentley had now started on another scent— the edition of my poetical works, which, after telling him the difficulties that at present beset the plan, I confessed to him was one I had so much at heart, that *whoever* would enable me to accomplish it should have my best wishes and co-operation, even though I myself should not gain a penny by it. I then told him the state of my poetical copyrights; *Lalla Rookh* and *The*

Melodies being in the hands respectively of the Longmans and Mrs Power, and the rest all my own, those of Carpenter having now returned to me. Was amused with the sanguineness with which, on hearing this (not having before known that so much of the property was my own), he seemed to consider the whole thing as settled, or, at least, settle-able without any difficulty. He would see Mrs Power and the Longmans on the subject, and had little doubt of bringing them round to his terms. Told him (while doubtfully shaking my head at all this confidence of his) how sanguine I had always found men of business in such matters; and that, in fact, I had constantly, in my dealings with them, been obliged to take the business line, and to repress as much as I could their "gay soarings." On more than one occasion have I endeavoured to keep the Longmans within bounds, as to the number of copies in an edition, when the event has proved that *I* was right not they. The imaginations, indeed, of some of your *matter-of-fact* men (as they are called) beat those of us poets hollow.

October 17 Bowles came after breakfast, more odd and ridiculous than ever. His delight at having been visited yesterday by the Prime Minister and Secretary of State, Lord L. having taken them both to Bremhill. He had left his trumpet at home, so that we could hardly make him hear, or, indeed, do anything with him but laugh. Even when he has his trumpet, he always keeps it to his ear while he is talking himself, and then takes it down when any one else begins to talk. To-day he was putting his mouth close to my ear, and bellowing away as if I was the deaf man, not he. We all pressed him to stay to dinner, but in vain; and one of his excuses was, "No, not indeed, I cannot; I must go back to Mrs Moore." Rogers very amusing afterwards about this mistake. "It was plain," he said, "where Bowles had been all this time; taking advantage of Moore's absence," &c. &c.

November 14 *to* 17 No change or novelty in my mode of existence; still the same still-life picture. It is some comfort, however, to find that, while so quiet at home, one has still the capability of kicking up a row abroad. Witness the "turn-up" I was the cause of the other night (the 21st) in the House of Commons. The subject of debate was the Pension List; and the best mode of recording what took place is to insert here the scrap from *The Times*' report of the debate:

An hon. member (name unknown, but with a strong Irish accent) rose to ask the Chancellor of the Exchequer a question. He wished to know whether the name of one Thomas Moore was in the list of pensions charged on the Civil List ("Oh, oh!"); and, if so, whether it was placed there for making luscious ballads for love-sick maidens, or for writing lampoons upon George IV. of blessed memory. (Cries of "Oh, oh!" and great confusion in the house.)

Mr Spring Rice—I am confident that the house, and I am equally persuaded that the public, will appreciate the motives which induced the Government to place the name of Thomas Moore on the Pension List. (Loud Cheers from both sides of the house.) By a formal resolution of this house, the Ministers of the day are authorised to grant these pensions as the reward of distinguished talent in literature and the arts. From the tones of his voice, I suspect that the hon. member

who has just put to me this extraordinary question belongs to
the same country with myself ("Hear," and a laugh). I believe
that there is no other Irishman but himself in this house—
differing, as many of them do, from the political opinions of
Thomas Moore—who does not feel it to be a credit to our
common country that the name of "one Thomas Moore" is
on the Pension List. (Immense cheering.) For my own part,
I think that the name of Thomas Moore is in itself a credit
to the Pension List. (General cheering.) I may ask,—and,
I hope, without offence,—whether it was for writing works of
a very democratic character and tendency that the name of
Dr Robert Southey is placed on the same Pension List with
that of Thomas Moore? The name of both those distinguished
men are on that List, and are on it for the same reasons
(cheers); and I rejoice as heartily in seeing the name of Southey
there as I do in seeing the name of Moore (cheers continued).
Both are men of great and immortal talent. Both have added
to the literary pleasures and instruction of their age and
country (vociferous cries of "Hear"); and I rejoice that both
of them have received, though from rival administrations, the
rewards to which they are both so fully and so justly entitled."
(Cheering from all quarters of the House.)

In reference to the above the London *Standard* has
the following:

We observed with regret that a gentleman—we doubt not
with the best disposition—complained of Mr Moore's pension. Mr Moore's pension is a tribute to genius—a testimony
to the claims of one who, if not the first living poet, is certainly
not second to any with whom the present generation has lived.
With Scott and Southey Mr Moore completes the number
of the first-class British poets of the nineteenth century, and
it is idle to underrate the merit of his poetry, because of the
direction taken by his genius, as was the miserable effort to
depreciate Scott on account of the lowness of the pursuits of
his borderers. That Mr Moore has been a political writer,

as well as a poet, ought to be the last reason to objecting to the reward of his political (?) merits in a free country. Alas! for the freedom of Great Britain, when a divorce shall be effected between literature and politics,—when men of genius or learning shall find it injurious to come forward in all their power, and, according to their conscientious views, in defence of that constitution which is the business of every Briton. The democratical changes that we have lately made are bringing the empire, indeed, rapidly enough under the dominion of brute ignorance. Let us not accelerate the calamity by interdicting the arena of politics to genius and knowledge. Mr Moore has taken the wrong side; but this matters nothing; we are contending for a principle—a principle in which Conservatives are much more deeply interested, as a party, than any other party can be. Of the party that seeks to establish the ascendancy of truth and justice, literature is the natural ally. It is gratifying to us to be able to add that, his political bias apart, there is nothing in Mr Moore's character—amiable, and honourable, and consistent as it is,—which ought to exclude him from the benefit for which we contend.

May 22 Breakfasted at Milnes', and met rather a remarkable party, consisting of Savage Landor and Carlyle (neither of whom I had ever seen before), Robinson, Rogers, and Rice. Savage Landor a very different sort of person from what I had expected to find him; I found in him all the air and laugh of a hearty country gentleman, a *gros rejoui*; and whereas his writings had given me rather a disrelish to the man, I shall take more readily now to his writings from having seen the man.

September 22 The day not very favourable for our passage home (from Ireland); but I cannot expect to be lucky in everything. Encountered an odd scene on going on board. The packet was full of people coming to see friends off, and among others was a party of ladies who, I should think, had dined on board, and who, on my being made known to them, almost devoured me with kindness, and at length proceeded so far as to insist on each of them *kissing* me. At this time I was beginning to feel the first rudiments of coming *sickness* and the effort to respond to all this enthusiasm, in such a state of stomach, was not a little awkward and trying. However I kissed the whole party (about five, I think,) in succession, two or three of them being, for my comfort, young and good-looking, and was most glad to get away from them to my berth, which, through the kindness of the captain (Emerson), was in his own cabin. But I had hardly shut the door, feeling very qualmish, and most glad to have got over this osculatory operation, when there came a gentle tap at the door, and an elderly lady made her appearance, who said that having heard of all that had been going on, she could not rest easy without being also kissed as well as the rest. So, in the most respectful manner possible, I complied with the lady's request, and then betook myself with a heaving stomach to my berth.

January 18, 19 Received a letter one of these days from Mrs Shelley, who is about to publish an edition of Shelley's works, asking me whether I had a copy of his *Queen*,—that originally printed for private circulation; as she could not procure one, and took for granted that I must have been one of those persons to whom he presented copies. In answering that I was unluckily *not* one of them, I added, in a laughing way, that I had never been much in repute with certain great guns of Parnassus, such as Wordsworth, Southey, her own Shelley, &c. Received from her, in consequence, a very kind and flattering reply, in which she says, "I cannot help writing one word to say how mistaken you are. Shelley was too true a poet not to feel your unrivalled merits, especially in the department of poetry peculiarly your own,—songs and short poems instinct with the intense principle of life and love. Such, your unspeakably beautiful poems to Nea; such, how many others! One of the first things I remember with Shelley was his repeating to me one of your *gems* with enthusiasm. In short, be assured that as genius is the best judge of genius, those poems of yours which you yourself would value most, were admired by *none* so much as Shelley. You know me far too well not to know I speak the exact truth."

February 1 *to* 3 The same monotonous course of life, which leaves but little for journalising. Have again played the same trick upon Bessy, with respect to her supplies for the poor, as I have done more than once before,—have confidentially got Boyse to send her a five-pound note, as if from himself, for the poor of Bromham. It makes her happy without the drawback of knowing it comes from my small means, and, in the way she manages it, does a world of good.

June 1 Saw by the bills that my counterpart *Tim Moore* was to be acted once more, "by desire," this

evening, and resolved not to miss it. Went to the
Haymarket, and left word that I would come. Dinner
at Spottiswoodes', Mrs Robert Arkwright, Longmans,
&c. &c.; a very large party. Told Mrs S. that I must
leave her for a short time (not saying where I was going)
at half-past nine, but would positively return; she,
though a little distrusting me, very good-humoured
about it; her guests, however, on seeing me rise to
depart, warned her not to let me slip out of her hands,
as I was sure not to return. Got a swift cab, and rattled
off to the Haymarket (from Bedford Square no trifling
distance); but found they had told me too early an hour,
as the piece preceding *Tim Moore* was still not yet
finished. This rather *contrariant*; but I was well re-
warded for the effort, having been seldom more amused.
The instructions of the Blue lady to her sister Blues
(the scene laid too at Devizes), as to the manner in
which they were to receive the supposed poet; their
getting him to write in their albums, &c.; the old dandy
who is to cry "Dem'd foine" at everything the poet
utters; all very comical. The medley, too, which the
Blue lady sings, made out of the first lines of the
different "Irish Melodies," as well as of the first few
bars of each air, is exceedingly well contrived, and was
most tumultuously encored. When she came again, it
was with an entirely new selection from the "Melodies,"
equally well strung together. Altogether, between the
fun of the thing, and the flattering proofs it gave of the
intimate acquaintance of the public with me and my
country's songs, I was kept in a state between laughing
and crying the whole time. The best of it all, too, was,

that I enjoyed it completely *incog.*, being in a little nook of a box where nobody could get a glimpse of me. Dashed off again, before it was quite over, to Bedford Square, and found that already more than suspicions had begun to be entertained of my fidelity. Lost no time in making up for the delay by sitting down immediately after Mrs Arkwright, and singing, as well as the breathless bustle I had been in would let me.

June 15 Went to the British Museum, and, having been told that it was a holiday, asked for Panizzi, who was full of kindness, and told me the library should be at all times accessible to me, and that I should also have a room entirely to myself, if I preferred it at any time to the public room. He then told me of a poor Irish labourer now at work about the Museum, who, on hearing the other day that I was also sometimes at work there, said he would give a pot of ale to any one who would show me to him the next time I came. Accordingly, when I was last there, he was brought where he could have a sight of me as I sat reading; and the poor fellow was so pleased, that he doubled the pot of ale to the man who performed the part of showman. Panizzi himself seemed to enjoy the story quite as much as I did. Received a note from Montalembert, full of kind and well-turned praise, which I fear I have lost. Should have been glad to transcribe it here, along with those many other tributes which I feel the more gratified by from an inward consciousness that I but little deserve them. Yet this is what, to the world, appears vanity. A most egregious though natural mistake.

It is the really self-satisfied man that least minds or cares what others think of him.

August 2 [IN LONDON] ... Dined at Lansdowne House. A dinner of men only, Lady L. being at Bowood. Company: Macaulay, Lord Clarendon, Lord Clanricarde, Rogers, young Fortescue, and Fonblanque. Sat between Macaulay and Rogers. Of Macaulay's range of knowledge anything may be believed, so wonderful is his memory. His view of Göthe as being totally devoid of the moral sense as well of real feeling; his characters, therefore, mere abstractions, having nothing of the man in them, and, in this respect, so unlike Schiller's. Such at least, as far as I could collect it, was his view of Göthe. Some conversation with Fonblanque, who, in speaking to me of my own writings, remarked how full of idiom they are. "There was in no writer (he said) so much idiom." This odd enough, as I told him, considering that I am an Irishman. Take for granted, however, that he had chiefly my lighter, playful style of writing in his mind.

September 21 Went to Bowood to dinner. Found, besides those Lady L. had mentioned (Lady Cunliffe, Lady Morley, and Rogers), Lord John and his children, Lady Macdonald and Macaulay. The dinner and evening very agreeable. Macaulay wonderful; never, perhaps, was there combined so much talent with so marvellous a memory. To attempt to record his conversation one must be as wonderfully gifted with memory as himself.

July 1 *to* 6   Have just found the note my poor Bess wrote to me, in sending up to town Tom's bill upon me for £112. "I can hardly bring myself to send you the enclosed. It has caused me tears and sad thoughts, but to *you* it will bring these and hard *hard* work. Why do people sigh for children? They know not what sorrow will come with them. How *can* you arrange for the payment? and what could have caused him to require such a sum? Take care of yourself; and if you write to him, for God's sake let him know that it is the very last sum you will or *can* pay for him. My heart is sick when I think of you, and the fatigue of mind and body you are always kept in. Let me know how you think you can arrange this." The difficulties to which this bill of Tom's reduced me were considerable: and I had not been more than a week or two at home, when another bill of his, drawn upon me at three months, for £100., was sent to me for acceptance. This blow coming so quick after the other, was, indeed, most overwhelming. It seems on his arrival at Bombay, he found that his regiment had been ordered on active service, and he was accordingly obliged to provide such an outfit as would enable him to join it. I could not do otherwise, of course, than accept the bill; but how I am to pay it, when due, Heaven only knows.

May 11   Went to the Literary Fund Chambers to see what were the arrangements and where I was to be seated; having in a note to Blewett, the secretary, begged of him to place me near some of my own personal friends. Found that I was to be seated between

Hallam and Washington Irving. All right. By the bye, Irving had yesterday come to Murray's with the determination, as I found, not to go to the dinner, and all begged of me to use my influence with him to change this resolution. But he told me his mind was made up on the point; that the drinking his health, and the speech he would have to make in return, were more than he durst encounter; that he had broken down at the Dickens' Dinner (of which he was chairman) in America, and was obliged to stop short in the middle of his oration, which made him resolve not to encounter another such accident. In vain did I represent to him that a few words would be quite sufficient in returning thanks. "That *Dickens'* Dinner," which he always pronounced with strong emphasis, hammering away all the time with his right arm, *more suo*, "that *Dickens'* Dinner," still haunted his imagination, and I almost gave up all hope of persuading him. At last I said to him, "Well, now, listen to me a moment. If you really wish to distinguish yourself, it is by saying the fewest possible words that you will effect it. The great fault with all the speakers, *myself* among the number, will be our saying too much. But if you content yourself with merely saying that you feel most deeply the cordial reception you have met with, and have great pleasure in drinking their healths in return, the very simplicity of the address will be more effective from such a man, than all the stammered out rigmaroles that the rest of the speechifiers will vent." The suggestion seemed to touch him; and so there I left him, feeling pretty sure that I had carried my point. It is very odd that while

some of the shallowest fellows go on so glib and ready
with the tongue, men whose minds are abounding with
matter should find such difficulty in bringing it out.
I found that Lockhart also had declined attending this
dinner under a similar apprehension, and only consented
on condition that his health should not be given.

The best thing of the evening, (as far as *I* was concerned), occurred after the whole grand show was over.
Irving and I came away together, and we had hardly
got into the street, when a most pelting shower came
on, and cabs and umbrellas were in requisition in all
directions. As we were provided with neither, our plight
was becoming serious, when a common cad ran up to
me, and said, "Shall I get you a cab, Mr Moore? Sure,
ain't *I* the man that patronises your Melodies?" He
then ran off in search of a vehicle, while Irving and I
stood close up, like a pair of male caryatides, under the
very narrow projection of a hall-door ledge, and thought
at last that we were quite forgotten by my patron. But
he came faithfully back, and, while putting me into the
cab (without minding at all the trifle I gave him for
his trouble) he said confidentially in my ear, "Now,
mind, whenever you want a cab, Misthur Moore, just
call for Tim Flaherty, and I'm your man." Now, this
I call *fame*, and of somewhat a more agreeable kind
than that of Dante, when the woman in the street
found him out by the marks of hell-fire on his beard.
(See Ginguene.)

September 17 Company at Lady Holland's (besides
Rogers who took me), Sir James Kemp, Sir Stephen

Hammick, some foreign minister whose name I could not catch, and one or two more. Some talk with Allen, during which I asked him whether he did not sometimes feel wearied by the sort of effort it must be to keep up conversation during these evenings, and he owned that it was frequently a most heavy task, and that if he had followed his own taste and wishes he would long since have given up that mode of life. For myself (as I believe I told him), that Holland House sort of existence, though by far the best specimen of its kind going, would appear to me, for any continuance, the most wearisome of all forms of slavery; and the best result I find of my occasional visits to town is the real relish with which I return to my quiet garden and study, where, in the mute society of my own thoughts and books, I am never either offended or wearied.

April Received a letter from Whewell (*the* Whewell) relative to the statue of Lord Byron by Thorwaldsen, which it was intended to place in Westminster Abbey. "I do not know," says Whewell, "what is the present prospect of such an intention being realised, but have been told that some thoughts are entertained of finding another place for the statue. If this is so, allow me to ask whether the application would be favourably received, if either Lord Byron's College or his university were to request to have the honour of finding a worthy situation for this work of art. His College [Trinity] would be willing to place it in the library, a noble one built by Wren, 200 feet long, and containing at present, I believe, the best collection of sculpture portraits in

England by Roubiliac; the greater part, like Lord Byron, members of the College. You are aware that Lord B. formed at his college friendships which he valued through life; and he is still recollected with regard by resident members of the college. He would be among a crowd of admirers of his genius, and, I may add, the building is daily open to strangers, and is visited by all who visit any of the University sights. The other situation which I should wish to propose, if the College be refused, is the new Fitzwilliam Museum, a noble building intended as a museum of arts, and just erected from the designs of Basevi. This edifice will be ready for the reception of works of art in a few years, and if you and the Committee who have to direct the disposal of the statue were inclined to accede to such a request, I shall move our Fitzwilliam Syndicate to request that the work should be placed in the part of the Museum which is appropriated to statues."

March 12 Perishable nature of modern poetry.

"We have seen too much of the perishable nature of modern literary fame, to venture to predict to Mrs Hemans that hers will be immortal, or even of very long duration. Since the beginning of our critical career we have seen a vast deal of beautiful poetry pass into oblivion, in spite of our feeble efforts to recall or retain it in remembrance. The tuneful quartos of Southey are already little better than lumber; and the rich melodies of Keats and Shelley, and the fantastical emphasis of Wordsworth, and the plebeian pathos of Crabbe, are melting fast from the field of our vision.

The novels of Scott have put out his poetry. Even the splendid strains of Moore are fading into distance and dimness, except where they have been married to immortal music; and the blazing star of Byron himself is receding from its place of pride. We need say nothing of Milman, and Croly, and Atherstone, and Hood, and a legion of others, who, with no ordinary gifts of taste and fancy, have not so properly survived their fame, have been excluded by some hard fatality from what seemed their just inheritance. The two who have the longest withstood this rapid withering of the laurel, and with the least mark of decay on their branches, are Rogers and Campbell, neither of them, it may be remarked, voluminous writers, and both distinguished rather for the fine taste and consummate elegance of their writings, than for that fiery passion, and disdainful vehemence, which seemed for a time to be so much more in favour with the public."—*Criticism of Lord Jeffrey.*

    What thanks do we owe, what respects and regards
    To Jeffrey the old nursery-maid of us bards.
    Who, resolved, to the last, his vocation to keep,
    First whipped us all round and now puts us to sleep.

INDEX

References are made to the actual presence of the persons and also to anecdotes and criticisms in which they figure, but only the most important are indicated and no references are given when they merely make an appearance on the scene.

BOWLES, REV. WILLIAM LISLE, 1, 3, 10, 20, 47, 66, 72, 158, 201, 202
BRUMMEL, "BEAU," 19, 42, 134
BURKE, EDMUND, 7, 9, 10, 11, 61, 64
BYRON, LORD, 7, 17, 22, 24, 25, 26, 32, 34, 35, 36, 40–43, 59–66, 72, 75, 89, 90, 114–117, 121, 122, 125, 127, 129, 130, 135, 136, 143, 148, 186, 197

CANNING, GEORGE, 28, 29
COLERIDGE, SAMUEL TAYLOR, 50, 51, 174, 176, 177, 186
COOPER, FENIMORE, 133
CRABBE, REV. GEORGE, 19, 58

DICKENS, CHARLES, 198, 211

GIFFORD, WILLIAM, 17

HAZLITT, WILLIAM, 27, 36
HOGG, JAMES ("ETTRICK SHEPHERD"), 96, 97
HOLLAND, LORD, 3–7, 17, 38, 39, 41, 64, 74, 129, 146
HOLLAND, LADY, 3, 24, 40, 175, 181

JEFFREY, FRANCIS, 55, 94, 98, 214, 215

LAMB, CHARLES, 50, 51, 64, 164
LANDOR, WALTER SAVAGE, 204
LANSDOWNE, LORD, 11, 47, 48, 58, 59, 65, 68, 196
LEWIS, MONK, 4

INDEX

MACAULAY, THOMAS BABINGTON, 157, 158, 165, 209
MACKINTOSH, SIR JAMES, 20, 21, 67, 68, 172
MOORE, ELIZABETH ("BESSY"), 1, 8, 15, 16, 19, 21, 23, 27, 31, 32, 33, 37, 52, 53, 56, 65, 70, 75, 104, 124, 138–143, 146, 147, 151, 153, 159, 194, 195, 206, 210

ROBINSON, HENRY CRABB, 50, 166
ROGERS, SAMUEL, 8, 9, 11, 12, 13, 14, 19, 21, 43, 49, 52, 59, 60, 61, 107, 110, 121, 122, 131, 133, 145, 155, 161, 171, 174, 202

SCHLEGEL, WILLIAM VON, 36, 165, 166
SCOTT, SIR WALTER, 14, 29, 42, 49, 54, 58, 76–93, 97, 98, 104, 109, 110, 112, 113, 120, 130, 131, 155, 160, 174
SHELLEY, MARY, 63, 116, 117, 148, 205, 206
SHELLEY, PERCY BYSSHE, 43, 116, 148, 206
SHERIDAN, RICHARD BRINSLEY, 2, 3, 4, 6, 7, 8, 9, 13, 32, 64, 71
SIDDONS, MRS, 136, 137
SMITH, REV. SYDNEY, 52, 106, 107, 159, 167, 168, 175, 177, 178, 179, 181, 182, 183, 197, 198
SOUTHEY, ROBERT, 42, 74, 107, 186
STAËL, MADAME DE, 39, 161

TALLEYRAND, PRINCE, 33, 181

WILSON, JOHN ("CHRISTOPHER NORTH"), 95
WORDSWORTH, WILLIAM, 27–31, 49, 50, 81, 134, 135, 138, 175, 183–187, 199, 200

Cambridge: Printed by W. LEWIS *at the University Press*